**DESIGN
MUSEUM**

DESIGN

an essential introduction

Published in 2015 by Goodman Fiell
An imprint of the Carlton Publishing Group
20 Mortimer Street
London W1T 3JW

10 9 8 7 6 5 4 3 2 1

Text © Gareth Williams, 2015
Design © Carlton Books Ltd 2015

A CIP catalogue record for this book is available from the British Library.

ISBN 978 1 78313 012 2

Printed in China

Jacket Picture Credits
Front cover:
Outer circle (from top pink circle, clockwise): Photography by Peter Mallet; Thonet
GmbH, Frankenberg; Tiago da Fonseca; Nendo, photographed by Masayuki Hayashi; Jair
Straschnow; 3D Systems; photography by John Ross, courtesy Lovegrove Studio; Artek;
Industrial Facility www.retailfacility.co.uk; Will Shannon; Barber Osgerby; Brompton
Bicycle, photographed by Peter Hughs.

Middle circle (from top yellow circle, clockwise): Studio Hansje; Gear Wrench; Paley
Studios Archive; Wikimedia Commons; KGID; Masaya Yoshimura; Barber Osgerby;
designed by Jólan van der Wiel, photographed by Jac van der Wiel; design by Ben Wilson
& Jonathan Pooley, photographed by John Selby; Original1227™©Anglepoise®; Petr
Krejci; Goodwin Hartshorn; photography by Daniel Alexander.

Inner circle (from top purple circle, clockwise): www.sugru.com; Private Collection;
Made in Mind www.madeinmind.co.uk; courtesy F.A.T Lab and Sy-Lab; Eone
Timepieces; Konstantin Grcic, for Vitra, photography by Marc Eggimann; Dyson; Dualit;
Melissa Shoes; Nendo, photographed by Masayuki Hayashi; Nissan; Anton Alvarez;
Benjamin Hennig www.londonmapper.org.uk.

Spine:
Vibol Moeung/Plumen.

Back cover (from top to bottom):
Design by Ben Wilson & Jonathan Pooley, photography by John Selby; 3D Systems;
Barber Osgerby.

DESIGN MUSEUM

DESIGN
an essential introduction

GARETH WILLIAMS

GOODMAN FIELL

CONTENTS

PREFACE

For the Design Museum, design matters because it is a means to understand the world around us. It is about making good use of technology and manufacturing techniques, but it is most of all about understanding people, the things they need, and the things they want. Design is about solving problems, but it's also about how we live.

It's about understanding function in the widest sense: people have emotional needs, as well as practical ones. A car is only partly a means of getting from one place to another. It has unintended consequences too. It can cause pollution, destroy cities, and trigger accidents. It can also look beautiful and become a cherished collector's piece.

Terence Conran, who founded the Design Museum which opened in 1989, always says that to design something, you have to know how to make it. Design is about being clear. The great Italian designer Vico Magistretti would tell students that drawings were all very well, but they hadn't really finished designing something until they could describe it over the telephone.

Design as we know it, has its roots in the Industrial Revolution, when the connection between the maker and the user, between the craftsman and the client, was broken by the introduction of machines that could produce hundreds and thousands of identical objects quickly. Setting up a craft workshop required an investment mainly in time and skill, while starting a factory was far more costly. Each individual handmade object would be as expensive to produce as the first, while the factory could produce objects that once the initial investment had been paid off cost very little.

The role of the designer emerged as an intermediary between manufacturer and user. The designer worked not with one individual user in mind, but with the needs of many people. And because they worked mostly for manufacturers, they had to understand what would sell, as well as what people needed.

Technology has moved on rapidly since the first steam powered production lines. The digital explosion has changed our relationship with our possessions, as the smart phone has taken over the tasks that were once performed by dozens of different analogue objects – cameras, music players, lap tops, maps, books, toys, and many others. And digital objects have few of the moving parts that used to give designers a starting point in understanding how to give them meaning and shape.

At the same time, production techniques such as additive manufacturing (as 3d printing is sometimes known) are displacing not just old style factories, but can allow the user to become their own designer, and manufacturer.

But what makes design so interesting is that it is continually adapting and changing to respond to these changes.

Deyan Sudjic, Director, Design Museum.

FOREWORD

This publication is an educational resource that invites readers to delve into the creative, pragmatic and essentially optimistic world of design and encounter some of the most ingenious and inspiring designs of today. It will take you behind the surface to explore the why and the how of design, and its' impact in shaping today's complex world. From an educational perspective, tutors, teachers and students will gain a breadth of context to enrich and expand teaching and learning about, through and in design. From Marco Polo to Barber Osgerby, Charles Darwin to fixperts, foaming porcelain to luffa nets, there is something to surprise and engage the curious mind and inspire the agile hand. A rich array of exemplar designs and case studies offer reach and depth of insight into the real world of professional design practice, from client brief, to studio context, manufacturing and production. In keeping with the Design Museum's learning programmes, teaching design literacy through experiential and contextual approaches which connect learners with multi-disciplinary and international designers, design practice and the material culture of design, the text also promotes a critical and reflective approach to individual responsibility both as producer and consumer in a world bursting with ideas, but groaning under the weight of stuff. This book aims to enthuse, provoke and inform future designers, engineers, technologists, manufacturers and educators through introducing cutting-edge, contemporary practice underpinned where relevant with historical context, helping shape and create the next generation of young people who can design the kind of future we know we need, in which design is an active force for good, for all. And who knows, perhaps future editions will feature your work too!

Dr Helen Charman, Director of Learning and Research, Design Museum.

WHAT IS DESIGN?

It may seem curious to ask, "What is design?" because we all feel we are, in some sense, design experts. This is because we buy and consume products that have been designed and manufactured, and we have strong views about what we like and dislike. Since the Industrial Revolution in the late eighteenth century, the term "design" has become most closely associated with the activity of giving shape and decoration to mass-produced goods in order to make them more appealing to consumers. This book is not a history of design; instead it looks closely at designing as an activity today and the role it plays in society. So perhaps we should be asking, "What is design *about*?", "What is design *for*?" and perhaps even "Who are designers, and what do they do?"

What connects all designers – whether they are designing an office chair, a bicycle suitable for carrying cargo, a dress for the Paris catwalk or the next generation of electric vehicle – is the belief that design can make a tangible improvement to the world in which we live. The activity of designing is essentially optimistic and forward-looking, because it embodies a belief that we can make the world of tomorrow better than the world we inherited from yesterday. From the earliest hand tools to the latest probes for exploring deep space, throughout history humankind has designed appliances that make us stronger, more adept and more able to control our environment to our advantage, driven by a mix of curiosity, arrogance and idealism.

Most commonly we make the error of thinking that design is only concerned with the look and feel of the finished product, whether that is a new pair of trainers

XL XBEAM SPANNER

Commonly the design of spanners and wrenches aligns both ends, but this range of wrenches designed by Richard Macor rotates the tool by 90 degrees in the centre. This simple change apparently increases the hand contact area by 500 per cent, making it much easier to use. Hand tools are designed to be extensions and enhancements to what we can do by hand, and design can contribute greatly to their efficiency.

RIGHT:
XL XBeam spanner
Designed by Richard Macor, Proprietary Technologies Inc.,
Manufactured by Gear Wrench®, USA, 2008

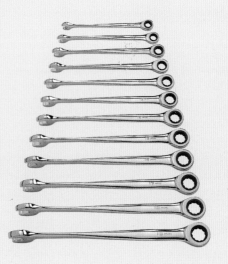

or a chair. It is true that a great deal of design effort is invested in making sure products appeal to us in their box-fresh state, at the moment we choose to buy them, but the best products are those where the designer has thought carefully more about how they will be made and how we will use them once they are ours. In fact, as this book will seek to reveal, design is a rigorous process of evaluation and testing, undertaken by professional expert designers who possess a complex skill-set including the abilities to "think outside the box" and to juggle contradictory information, as well as intimate knowledge of the constraints and opportunities offered by the materials and techniques at their disposal.

Put plainly, design is a problem-solving process. And what are the problems designers seek to resolve? These are varied but may include big questions such as how to make products more efficient and which have less impact on the environment, and more specific issues such as how to make this season's products distinctive from rivals and from last season's collection. In some cases the solution will appear to be almost obvious and intuitive, but will bring a huge improvement to an existing product, for example the XL XBeam Spanner.

BELOW:
Donky bike
Designed by Ben Wilson,
Manufactured by Donky Bike,
UK, 2013

Design looks forward and also outward: it is seldom undertaken solely for the benefit of the designer. Unlike fine art, which tends towards a personal quest for meaning and expression on behalf of the artist, design is outward-looking and not introspective. Designers usually anticipate that many people will experience and benefit from their work. For this reason, designing is a complex activity; it requires a leap of imagination by the designer to consider how the uninformed user will respond to their work. Designing is often collaborative, especially for complex products such as electronic goods or vehicles. Designers need to be able to work with specialists from other fields, such as material scientists, computing experts, engineers, manufacturers and marketers, to name but a few. In these cases, the designer may remain anonymous but is directing the process of realizing ideas as objects and outcomes. For example, every aspect of a car is heavily designed, yet very few car designers are household names because by necessity it is a collaborative activity.

So, design sets out to solve problems, often collaboratively, and is an inherently optimistic activity. Design is also a way of communicating ideas. Information is designed in print media like this book, in newspapers and magazines, signage and wayfinding, websites, branding and even the look of film, television and stage shows. In these examples designers are organizing our thoughts and opinions, and giving structure to the world around us. This can be as mundane as public-service films made to encourage public safety, but if these are well designed the message can be very memorable, for example the animation made for the Melbourne metro system to reinforce safe behaviour around the train system. This short film called *Dumb Ways to Die*, complete with a catchy song and endearing characters, has been viewed over 85 million times on YouTube. Sometimes even the design of signage can communicate a secondary message, such as the type family designed for signage at Castledown Primary School in Hastings, England, that simultaneously instructs pupils how to form their own writing.

We may also ask ourselves, "Why does design matter? Why should I care about it?" The answer is simply that design completely surrounds us and we live in an entirely man-made world; just as we seek to understand nature, so too we need to comprehend the world we are shaping for ourselves. In this sense design becomes a moral activity because (let's face it) we are all aware of the damage wrought by profligate consumption of poorly-designed and wasteful products. The design profession itself is implicated because it was designers who first conceived of "planned obsolescence" whereby products were intentionally made with short-lived components or passing, faddish appearances that quickly dated, leading to their swift replacement with the latest models.

Almost everything we experience has been designed, and not only the myriad products that we buy. It is possible to talk about the design of services and systems, such as welfare, education and health, often informed by political and economic dogmas but nonetheless containing a belief in their capacities to deliver progress and create a better world. These are somewhat intangible ideas and politicians rely on designers to help express them, for example the eye-catching poster designed by street artist Shepard Fairey to support Barack Obama's first presidential campaign

RIGHT:
**Castledown Primary School
type family**
Designed by Anthony Sheret,
Edd Harrington and Rupert Dunk,
UK, 2012

CASTLEDOWN

AaBbCcDd (A)

AaBbCcDd (B)

AaBbCcDd (C)

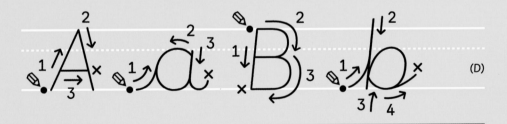
(D)

(E)

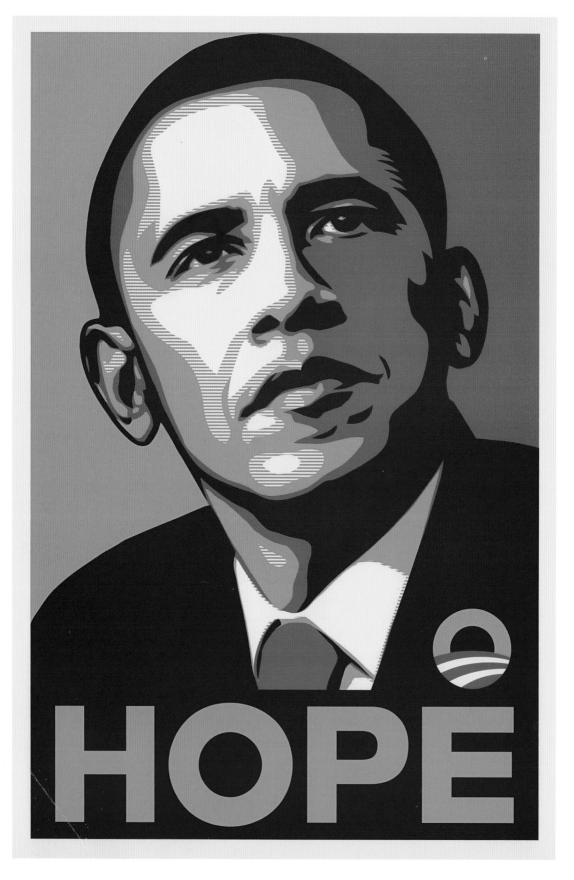

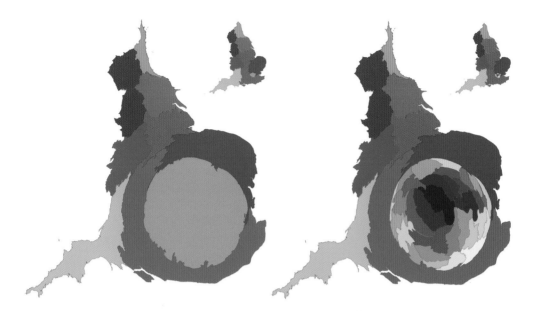

in 2008. The built environment of our towns and cities and the transport networks that link them are designed, as are vast engineering projects such as hydroelectric dams and nuclear power stations: the essential infrastructures of modern life arise from the problem-solving design process. Projects like the London Mapper translate hard data about the city into visually complex and arresting diagrams to communicate things about the vast metropolis that generally we cannot see.

Visually rich and seductive, the world of mass entertainment, from cinema to theme parks, television to popular magazines and gaming, is enriched and formed by design thinking and innovation too, as is the virtual world of the Internet by digital design. But woven into these megalithic social, commercial and even nation-sized design activities are our own personal design choices. We design our own living spaces and project our identities by designing our personal appearances through the clothes, haircuts and accessories we choose. We could even say that through cooking we are designing our own food.

In this book we will focus on design associated with industrial mass production with particular emphasis on the consumer goods and experiences that shape the world for many of us. First, we will look in detail at how design arises; at design briefs and the processes of answering them. The key attributes of designed objects will be discussed next, including the importance of functionality and the choices designers make regarding appearance and style. We will consider the role of the consumer in shaping industrially made products through customization and use. At some length, the principal materials and techniques used to make products will be examined, as well as future challenges and opportunities for designers. Lastly, through a series of case studies we will see how incremental evolution of design ideas and innovation transform some archetypal product types, as well as looking in detail at some designs that break entirely new ground.

OPPOSITE:
Barack Obama campaign poster
Designed by Shepard Fairey, USA, 2008

ABOVE:
London Mapper website
Designed by Professor Danny Dorling, School of Geography and the Environment, Oxford University, UK, www.londonmapper.org.uk 2014

1. WHAT IS A DESIGN BRIEF?

All designing is a problem-solving process and the design brief is the starting point, in a sense the action plan or route map that will help the designer to respond to the issue. The brief both identifies the problem and suggests an answer. It is a dynamic, live document to which the designer will return at stages during the design process to assess progress against the original aims. It contains both constraints and limitations, but also opportunities for innovations and discoveries. And it can act like a contract, detailing the responsibilities and expectations of the designer and their client, often a manufacturer.

Designing is problem-solving because designers are seeking to improve situations or answer needs. Sometimes the task is to improve an existing design, like the Seaboard (see opposite); at other times the problem may be one arising from particular requirements, such as the design of homewares for the physically impaired. In the latter instance, the problems may be practical, such as finding the optimum handle to be gripped by an arthritis sufferer. Alternatively, the problem could be symbolic, for example ensuring that people who are visually impaired do not feel stigmatized by the products designed for their use. The problem that is identified in the brief may even be the race to fill an emerging market opportunity, such as the sudden demand for smart phones after the launch of the Apple iPhone.

The brief sets out the parameters of the design exercise that will be undertaken. Some of the examples in this book are speculative self-generated briefs composed by the designers alone, but most are a collaborative exercise between the designer and their client, who is usually a manufacturer. Perhaps the designer has had an idea for a product and has sought out a manufacturer with certain skills or access to a particularly suitable market in the hope that they will take it on. Many furniture designers, for example, work independently as freelancers and may produce work for a number of different manufacturers. Alternatively, a manufacturer may take a look at their existing product range and determine that it could be improved by adding a certain type of new product.

Whether the designer or the manufacturer initiates the project, it becomes defined by the brief. The brief will pose the challenge, which may be something like "design a new chair for us". But a chair can be made in many different ways using numerous materials, all of which have cost implications that will determine not only how it will be made but where in the market it will be positioned. Therefore, the brief will need to be more specific: it may be "design a new chair for us that will be made of plastic". Plastic, as we will explore in more depth later

THE SEABOARD

An accomplished musician himself, Roland Lamb conceived the Seaboard, a revolutionary soft and flexible musical instrument interface, because he detected a limitation in the existing paradigm of a piano keyboard: that is, each key only produces a single note. The Seaboard, on the other hand, enables players to slide between notes, creating entirely new musical possibilities. But without the centuries of development underpinning the existing keyboard paradigm, we would have no Seaboard. The brief Lamb set himself was based on an intimate understanding of the existing keyboard, and an imaginative leap concerning what it could become. This required him to master electronics and material science, which enabled him to perfect the sensor-embedded silicone keyboard that in turn optimized its playability.

BELOW:
Seaboard Grand electronic keyboard
Designed by Roland Lamb and Hong-Yue Edom,
Manufactured by ROLI, UK, 2013

DESIGNS FOR THE VISUALLY IMPAIRED

Designed with the best intentions, nevertheless many products that aim to aid the visually impaired remain unpopular. This is because these products favour high visibility colours, large bold graphics and simplified, readable forms in a bid to enhance their functionality. Unfortunately these features can also make appliances like kitchenware or telephones look like toys and their users can feel patronized or even infantilized. People with poor sight do not wish attention to be drawn to their impediment by garish, childlike products. The designers' challenge, therefore, when they compose a design brief, is to understand the perspective of the intended users and design accordingly. Moreover, the best examples of these types of products are those designed for everyone with less obvious attention to the special needs of a few. These are inclusive designs that counter the stigmatizing tendency of too many products designed for people with disabilities.

The Bradley Timepiece is a tactile watch designed for blind people that nevertheless has great appeal to design-aware consumers with sight. Its innovation is that the hands are replaced by touchable ball-bearings that rotate around the face. The brief recognized the way in which the blind explore their surroundings through touch while also ensuring the watch had broad appeal. It was named after and developed with Bradley Snyder, a US naval officer who lost his sight in Afghanistan in 2011 who subsequently won swimming medals at the London Paralympic Games in 2012.

More examples of inclusive design are discussed in Chapter 7.

ABOVE:
Bradley Timepiece wristwatch
Designed by Eone Timepieces Inc., USA, 2013

in the book, has properties that lend it to the mass-manufacture of products with a tendency to low individual unit costs because of economies of scale. It is not ideal for making highly crafted one-off or limited-edition pieces. So our brief may have further clarification: "design a new chair for us that we will make of plastic from a single moulding, so that it will be quickly and efficiently produced in vast numbers". Even further parameters can be set by the brief, for example to use a newly invented type of plastic or to ensure it can be sold for a certain price. Very quickly it is apparent that quite tight parameters have been set for the type of chair to which the designers must aspire.

A different instance of setting a brief may come from a commission or other third-party arrangement, such as the brief given to Barber Osgerby to design the relay torch, prepared by the organizing committee of the London 2012 Olympic Games. This is explored in much more depth in the next chapter, but it is worth mentioning here because it shows how a brief may also represent the requirements of very many stakeholders. In this instance there was the International Olympic Committee's need for the torch to communicate the symbolic values of the games worldwide, as well as local practical requirements such as ensuring the torch stayed alight in Britain's notoriously rainy weather. Symbolism and functionality are very different concerns, but both can shape a design brief.

The best design briefs are those that make very clear all the practical, technical and other constraints with which a designer will have to contend, without stifling any chance of a creative response. They establish how a design will benefit the manufacturer and identify who will be the market. They show awareness of context, which could be the state of existing competition that must be bettered or the opportunities presented by an emerging technology or market. Lastly, and importantly, both the client and the appointed designer understand them: briefs can act like contracts that spell out the expectations of both parties.

THE MYTO CHAIR

The MYTO chair shows how several partners working together can develop a design brief, in this instance the chemical producer BASF, the designer Konstantin Grcic and the manufacturer Plank. Each partner brought with them their own expertise and their own hopes for the outcome.

The project was initiated in the summer of 2006 by the German chemical giant BASF, which had developed a new plastic compound they called Ultradur® High Speed – chemical name polybutylene terephthalate (PBT) – a strong, heat-resistant material that also has the property of flowing well through moulds. It was designed primarily for use in technical engineering and components such as fuse boxes; scarcely visible products. BASF makes materials, not consumer products, so in order to promote Ultradur the company sponsored presentation days to introduce the material to selected designers, ultimately leading to a commission for Munich-based Konstantin Grcic to design an application. They chose Grcic because of his record of designing challenging and innovative furniture with a sculptural sensibility. BASF's intention for the design brief was to gain high visibility for its new material by applying it to a startling product made ready for the market, not made only for public relations purposes.

Cantilevered chairs have only two legs, usually at the front, capable of supporting the seat and back. They seem illogical but many were designed from the 1920s onwards exploiting the structural capabilities of tubular stainless steel. Danish designer Verner Panton designed one of the most famous cantilevered chairs in the 1960s, a single plastic moulding known as the Panton chair, but since then very few have been attempted. Grcic determined to exploit Ultradur's strength to design a new cantilevered plastic chair. The design brief required him to acknowledge previous cantilevered chairs but not imitate them. His greatest challenge was to work out how little Ultradur he could use to create a strong yet light chair.

Grcic introduced the Italian manufacturer Plank to the project to make the chair. A small family-run firm making chairs for four generations, since the 1990s Plank had transformed itself from a traditional maker into a specialist in advanced technologies. The new chair would, it was hoped, help to secure Plank's place as a major manufacturer of multi-functional, stackable chairs, while a cantilevered chair, manufactured as a single moulding, would challenge BASF's claims for Ultradur's strength and malleability.

Once the partners were in place and the goal established, each developed the brief according to their expertise. Grcic, with his studio KGID, used foam models and other mock-ups to develop the overall form of the chair. He allowed the structural necessities of a cantilevered chair to determine the overall shape: the frame was thicker where it was required to be stronger and a perforated seat evolved to use less material and lend the chair transparency. BASF undertook extensive computer-aided testing of Grcic's design concept to understand how Ultradur would perform, including analysis of how the material would flow through the mould, ultimately developing the material specifically to suit the demands of the chair. After the partners had agreed the overall form, Plank were able to use the designers' data to make the first full-scale 3D sintered prototypes that informed the mould-making process. For injection-moulded products like the MYTO chair, the mould is the single most expensive aspect and all parties must be satisfied the product will work before it is made.

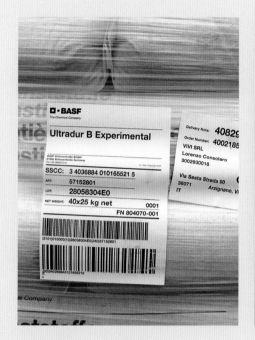

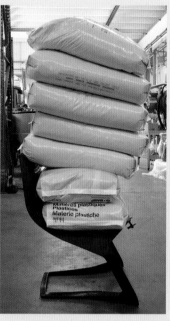

ABOVE LEFT:
Labelling for Ultradur
BASF, Germany, 2006

ABOVE RIGHT:
First off-tool Myto chair being tested
Plank, Italy, 2007

LEFT:
Early model of the Myto chair
KGID, Germany, 2006

WHAT IS A DESIGN BRIEF?

Working at full speed, the partners had designed, developed and fabricated the first examples of the chair made in Ultradur by the middle of 2007, to present at the world's largest plastics trade fair in Düsseldorf. These first chairs allowed further development of the design, the mould and the material in order for Plank to push ahead with market-ready production models of the chair for its launch at the Milan Furniture Fair in April 2008. One of the most noticeable aspects of the finished chair is the colour, which communicates so strongly yet was one of the last details to be considered since it had no bearing on the major structural and production challenges of the design.

LEFT:
Tooling for the Myto Chair
Plank, Italy, 2007

ABOVE:
**Konstantin Grcic (left) with production
versions of the Myto Chair**
Plank, Italy, 2007

2. WHAT IS THE DESIGN PROCESS?

Once a brief has been agreed, designers must work out a strategy to respond to it most effectively. There is no single "right way" to go about the design process. Some designers immerse themselves in extensive research of markets, contexts, rival propositions, materials and manufacturing processes: anything that may make them better informed and more likely to propose the best solution. Others may choose a much more intuitive and personal response, following their own tastes and interests. A very productive response to any design brief is one of curiosity and wonder about how it can be answered, and many designers in all disciplines make collections of objects and images that act as libraries of ideas on which they can call for inspiration. Many fashion or graphic designers begin their work by creating "mood boards" of inspirational and informative images, textures and colours, and these may be useful for designers in other areas too, such as product designers.

Whatever the varied approaches may be, the responses to a design brief will share similarities. They will be iterative processes, meaning that they will repeat and refine stages of the response and evaluate them at each step, possibly through sketching or modelling, and at later stages by creating full-scale mock-ups and testing materials likely to be used in the final product, as we saw with the development of the MYTO chair (see Chapter 1). Much of the design process may be thought of as experimental, and in science an experiment has an expected outcome and can be tested against known data. Design experiments should be no different and at each experimental stage a designer must be clear what they are testing and how they will measure its success. Much of this can be drawn from how well the design meets the criteria of the brief. So the design brief remains an active document because it stands as a yardstick against which to evaluate the success of the design response, and as a reminder of the core purposes of the project, which can be forgotten or overlooked by designers when they become embroiled in fascinating details.

The rest of this chapter will look in depth at the design process behind a very well-known success, the London 2012 Olympic torch, designed by the London-based studio Barber Osgerby.

As with most high-profile, publicly funded projects, the design of the London Olympics was largely commissioned by inviting designers to compete for various aspects of the event. The briefs were set by LOCOG, the London Organising Committee of the Olympic Games, the body with responsibility to deliver all aspects of the project. Ed Barber and Jay Osgerby founded their studio in 1996 and now front an organization of about 70 designers and architects with an international roster of high-end furniture and product brands as clients. As a

ABOVE:
Image board for the Olympic relay torch in the studio
Barber Osgerby, UK, 2011

general rule of thumb they do not enter competitions (which are time-consuming and reactive, rather than proactive and creative processes), but they were looking out for such opportunities for the London Olympics. LOCOG advertised for expressions of interest in designing the relay torch by laying out the broad context of the project. This was not a design brief as such, and its aim was to enable the organizers to determine whether a studio was sufficiently experienced and capable of taking on the project. Perhaps one thousand expressions of interest were received, which were whittled down to 50 and finally a shortlist of five, with the Design Council advising LOCOG on its selection.

Only at this stage was a detailed brief issued to the selected designers, who were then given just 10 days to compose a detailed design and manufacturing plan. Like many designers, the time pressure focused their minds because, as Jay Osgerby told me, "If there is pressure you get the job done". The Olympic torch relay is a highly symbolic part of the festival, as the torches bring the Olympic flame from Mount Olympus in Greece (the site of the ancient games) to the next host city via a complicated running tour around the host nation. The flame is regarded as almost sacred, and each torch is lit from the previous torch in the relay. Therefore the torch must include certain design references to the values and symbols of the Olympics, and fit in with, but simultaneously stand out from, the history of Olympic torches. At their studio the designers assembled image boards showing

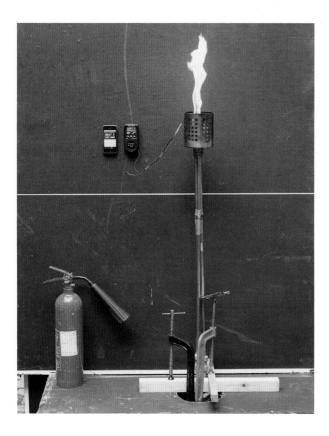

LEFT:
Prototype to test the strength of the flame
Barber Osgerby, UK, 2011

RIGHT:
Early blue foam prototypes to determine the overall form
Barber Osgerby, UK, 2011

inspirational forms, structures, materials and processes, for example numerous ways to fold, pleat and perforate sheet materials. Among the inspirational images were sketches of ideas and details that gradually coalesced into the recognizable shape of the torch as we know it.

The most important part of the design brief was to ensure that the flame does not go out, and the brief document was filled with data about weather conditions in Britain's notoriously turbulent summer. Keeping the flame intact was the prime constraint of the brief, but so too was making sure the torch was portable for the 8,000 volunteers who would each carry one torch for a mile during the relay. So the brief required both an aesthetic and a practical design response.

Barber Osgerby observed various trilogies in the brief: London is the only city to have hosted the modern Olympics three times (in 1908, 1948 and 2012); there are three stated Olympic values "Friendship, Respect and Excellence"; and three parts to the Olympic motto "Faster, Higher, Stronger". With this in mind the designers structured the torch around a triangular core with a flared, triangular head to accommodate the gas cylinder and burner. The triangulated form symbolized these trilogies, gave the torch good tensile strength and was settled very early in the design process, as is apparent in the very earliest blue foam models, made in the studio at full size. Easy and cheap to make, blue foam models are frequently made at the early stages of the design process as they help designers to determine the volume and outline of their product.

To reduce the weight and allow for the flame to be ventilated but also shielded, the designers came up with a perforated pattern of holes in a double-layer structure: over 7,000 holes in each torch. The holes created a repeating intersecting pattern of rings, rather like the Olympic logo multiplied indefinitely. Later the number of holes was adjusted to match the 8,000 volunteer runners and the number of torches that would have to be made for them. This detail gave the torch specific relevance to the London Olympics while the other symbolic elements referred to the Olympic movement as a whole.

At this stage of the design process the designers were still in competition, although the shortlist had reduced to just two studios. Barber Osgerby wanted to make the torches using 3D printing (a relatively new process discussed in more depth in Chapter 8) as this would mean they could be made in the UK using a technology in which Britain excelled, but in awarding them the commission the clients insisted they rethink this.

By now the torch was little more than a proposed shape bearing symbolic messages, with no indication of its material, or if the design met the stringent testing criteria. The designers entered an intense period of design development, often necessitating collaboration with specialist consultants and collaborators such as engineers and the company that made and tested the gas burners. All kinds of prototypes were made to test different aspects of the design, for example the size and positioning of the ventilation holes to ensure even the strongest winds or downpours would not extinguish the flame. Some of these were rudimentary tests by the design team itself and the look and feel of the prototypes was

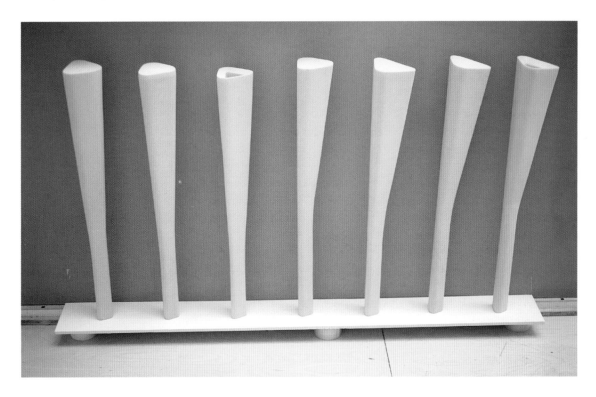

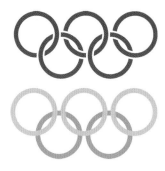

LEFT:
Development of the hole pattern
showing its relationship to the
Olympic logo
Barber Osgerby, UK, 2012

OPPOSITE:
Parts of the Olympic relay torch
in sequence during fabrication,
from laser cutting the aluminium,
through folding and welding
the sheets, to the gold-plated
finished version
2012

unimportant as the tests were technical. Later on very extreme testing of more
refined prototypes took place in the all-weather wind tunnel facility at BMW in
Munich. Alongside physical models, the team used computer design software
that enabled them to model stress tests such as the liable impact if the torch was
dropped. They developed a computer algorithm to resize and reposition the 8,000
holes as the overall form was constantly adjusted and tweaked as a result of other
tests and refinements. The computer files became the final design that could be
communicated to the client and to the fabricators.

The designers took the decision to make the body of the torch from aluminium,
rather than 3D print it. Working with specialist metalworkers in Coventry, they
developed a way to laser-cut the sheet metal before folding it to create the form, at
which point the seam was laser-welded and additional holes cut to disguise it and
complete the decoration. In total, an incredible 64 million aluminium discs were
cut during the fabrication of the torches, all of which could be easily recycled.

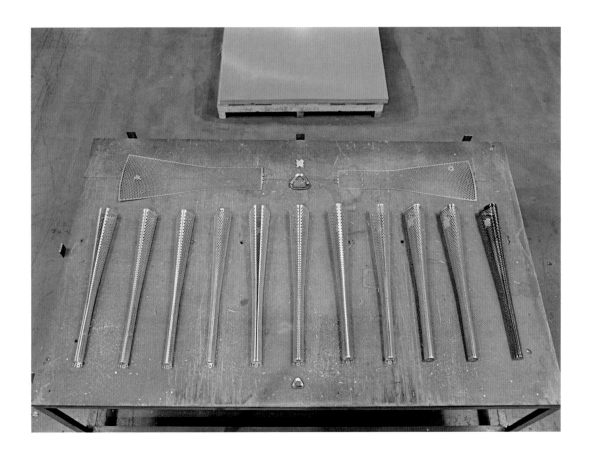

The development of the Olympic torch was a fast project lasting about 18 months from the launch of the competition to the staging of the relay. The designers agreed that the tight time frame and extreme constraints, both technical and aesthetic, aided their process as these gave them plenty to respond to. Perhaps because of the project's speed, there was a small opportunity for creative thinking early in the project lasting only about 10 days, and decisions made then had to be right. In this respect, the designers needed to trust to their experience and intuition that they could solve some unknown aspects later on, for example what materials and techniques they would use to make the torch. The process also conflated the design of the torch with determining how it would be fabricated, and the designers relied heavily on their collaborators' expertise to develop special techniques, such as the folding and welding jig.

The final design detail of the torch was to determine its surface finish. The designers wanted it to look more like a specialist piece of sports equipment than a

ABOVE:
The Olympic torch relay
UK, 2012

LEFT:
CAD model showing the location of the burner and gas canister
Barber Osgerby, 2012

trophy, and they achieved this through its smooth, clean profile and highly engineered detailing. Yet the gold-plated surface also seems appropriate as bearing the torch in the relay was the time for each runner to shine.

Every design project will require its own unique design process, but they all have similarities. Each brief requires the designer to become (to some degree) an expert in the field by acquainting him- or herself with the contexts and constraints of the particular project: Barber Osgerby had to ensure it understood its client's expectations and quickly learned about the other torches that had been designed for earlier relays. The creative part of the process was short and finite, and the designers of the torch eagerly sought inspiration and comparison wherever they could find it. The ability to express early ideas as sketches and models is essential to communicating design thinking without words. These ideas quickly resolved themselves into more sophisticated models and computer renderings to explore aesthetics, proportions, volume and balance. At the same time, other tests were conducted on technical prototypes and computer models. The results of all the repeated tests informed the next generations of prototypes as the process advanced. Once their ideas were fixed and had been checked, the designers worked with their clients and an ever-broadening circle of specialist consultants and manufacturers to ensure the torch could be made on time, on budget and retain the original design ideas in response to the brief. Much of the design process, therefore, is a series of checks and measures, referring back to the brief to guarantee the project is still on track and looking ahead to how these ideas will be delivered.

Barber Osgerby's design process for the Olympic torch is unusual in that it had a very high profile and came with many constraints and requirements, but the same could be said of very many high-performing products in the modern world. What we can generalize from its experience is that the design process is seldom linear or conducted in isolation. More likely, the designer is both the creative force and the manager of the project, steering it through unexpected changes of course and working with myriad stakeholders and collaborators.

RIGHT:
The Olympic Torch
2012

3. FORM & FUNCTION

"It is the pervading law of all things organic and inorganic, of all things physical and metaphysical, of all things human and all things superhuman, of all true manifestations of the head, of the heart, of the soul, that the life is recognizable in its expression, **that form ever follows function**. *This is the law*."

Louis Sullivan
"The Tall Office Building Artistically Considered"
Lippincott's Magazine, 1896

"Form follows function," famously decreed the architect Louis Sullivan; modernist architects and designers during the twentieth century took his edict extremely seriously. Industrially made products should express how they were made by not concealing their structures behind unnecessary decoration, and their function should be obvious; they should be intuitive to use. This did not exclude any aesthetic considerations by designers, as the design writer John Gloag argued in the 1930s: "To imagine that beauty invariably resides in a piece of competent engineering and to assume that 'fitness for purpose' is the golden rule for the creation of beauty is to chain creative ideas to abject utility." He knew that if designers only focused on the function of their designs, the results might well lack any visual appeal. Products would only be tools. Undeniably there is beauty to be found in the design of good tools but, as the philosopher Martin Heidegger argued, a hammer is really an extension to an arm, and since the focus of the activity is on the nail, the hammer effectively becomes invisible. Good tools, therefore, should recede into the background and we should be aware of them only if they break down (because they were not made appropriately for their task: they were not "fit for purpose"); they get in the way of the job they purport to do (because they were not designed well enough); or we lose them (their absence makes us aware of the job that cannot be done without them). In this chapter we will explore the relationship of form and function, and the different ways in which designers approach the "rule" that one should follow the other.

Many utilitarian objects perfectly illustrate how their function dictates their form, and many are either vernacular designs that have evolved over long periods, or industrial products whose designers are anonymous. Wooden spoons, three-legged milking stools and ceramic storage jars are all refined-yet-simple examples of useful things that have been perfected over time with countless small variations by numerous makers and users; a paper clip is industrially made but we have forgotten who designed it.

RIGHT:
Traditional three-legged milking stool

PAPER CLIPS

The increase of trade and bureaucracy in the mid-nineteenth century led to the rise of paper-filled offices, and these papers needed to be sorted. Until this point, loose sheets were pinned together, with obvious risks and limitations, but the invention of malleable steel wire allowed the design of a much better solution: the paper clip. Paper clips work because they are like springs: they want to return to their original shape and have enough flexibility to allow them to be opened. Just a tiny twist of wire, the paper clip nevertheless perfectly embodies the law of physics that a force exerted on a spring returns with equal force. The Norwegian Johan Vaaler is sometimes credited with inventing the paper clip, which he patented in 1899, but many variants were patented around that time, some of which are known to be earlier. The most familiar form is known as the Gem, named after the British maker of paper-clip-making machines, Gem Manufacturing Ltd. It is estimated that each year some twenty thousand million paper clips are manufactured.

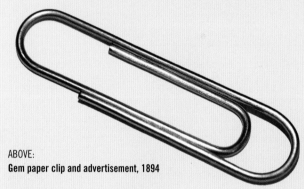

DON'T MUTILATE YOUR PAPERS
with pins or fasteners, but use the
✳GEM ✦ PAPER ✦ CLIP✳
Only satisfactory device for temporary attach-
ment of all kinds of papers. Quickly applied and removed.
25 Cents a Box.
Cushman & Denison, 172 9th Ave., N. Y.
Published in *The Book-Keeper*, Aug. 1894, p. 6. Discovered by The Early Office Museum (www.officemuseum.com)

ABOVE:
Gem paper clip and advertisement, 1894

BELOW:
Patented paper clips, clockwise from top left;
Wright, 1901; Reeve, 1897; Ringklip, 1910; McGill, 1900;
Wright, 1877; Eureka, 1894; Clipper, 1898; Banjo, 1903

LEFT:
Teapot
Designed by Marianne Brandt,
Manufactured by the
Bauhaus Metal Workshop,
Germany, 1924

Early modernist designers, such as those associated with the Bauhaus school in Germany during the 1920s, experimented with simple geometric shapes, often in combination, to construct new forms for items such as tableware and lamps. While these were most definitely breaks with the decorative traditions that had prevailed before the First World War, a vital point about functionalist design as we would understand it now was still absent. This is the relation of the object to its user. The form of an object is more than just the physical space it occupies, its volume or even the particularities of its shape. The designer also needs to think about how it will be made and used. So, while a geometric teapot may capture the spirit of modernity, it may not be easy to fabricate and may be difficult or even impossible to use. A later chapter will explore ergonomics and human-centred design in much more depth. In this context we need to bear in mind that the form of an object should be dependent on the way it is held, operated and otherwise used. After all, if designers are seeking to improve our lives and the ways in which we experience the world, how can they succeed if their designs don't actually work?

A comparison of several lamps will let us explore form and function in more detail, and show how Louis Sullivan's edict can be subverted without damaging the integrity of the product. The original Anglepoise desk lamps were designed by the British automotive engineer George Cawardine, exploiting a new type of helical spring he had patented in 1932. He specialized in designing suspension systems and his lamp similarly used springs in tension to position the adjustable lamp to face in almost any direction, making it a very versatile task light. The visible springs clearly express their function and the lamp can be regarded as an early example of a "high-tech" aesthetic celebrating engineering. The mechanics were also inspired by the natural world, specifically limb muscles: the lamp is like an outstretched arm.

In 2008 British designer Anthony Dickens designed a playful riposte to Cawardine's lamp called Fifty. Whereas the original Anglepoise lamp was adjustable in any direction, Dickens's lamp is fixed at an optimal angle of 50 degrees. And while the original lamp was a triumph of engineering and mechanics, Dickens simply cast his lamp in a single polycarbonate injection moulding. The electricity cord is positioned to recall the angled arm of Cawardine's original. Which is most functional? Cawardine wins on flexibility, but Dickens wins on simplicity. Ron Gilad appropriated the Anglepoise form to make a chandelier for the Dutch manufacturer Moooi, an ironic exercise where the lamp's adjustability and utility as a piece of office equipment were exaggerated and emphasized to become a decorative feature. Similarly, Gaetano Pesce played with the lamp's scale with his enormous Moloch floor lamp. Standing over two metres high, the Moloch dwarfs everything around it and plays with our sense of perspective. Another giant variant is the Brave New World lamp designed by the British studio Freshwest and manufactured by Moooi. It is made entirely of timber lengths that are pegged together in a seemingly haphazard and random, organic manner that pastiches the engineered character of Cawardine's original design. The designers claim to have been inspired by Far Eastern bamboo scaffolding. Cast-iron counterweights

OPPOSITE:
Anglepoise task light
Designed by
George Cawardine,
Manufactured by
Herbert Terry & Sons,
UK, 1933

BELOW:
Fifty task light
Designed by
Anthony Dickens,
Manufactured by
Anglepoise®, UK, 2008

take the role played by the springs in a conventional Anglepoise lamp. Last of all, Tiago da Fonseca made his version of the Anglepoise entirely of floppy rubber, utterly (and hilariously) subverting Cawardine's original concept and appropriately retitling the lamp as No Angle, No Poise.

In contrast, Ron Arad's 2007 PizzaKobra table light has all the flexibility of Cawardine's much-imitated archetype but the designer has found entirely new ways to achieve the same functionality. It looks like a flat coil of metal tube (a disc, inspiring the name "Pizza"), but hidden within the tube are invisible swivelling knuckle joints that enable it to be uncoiled and set in any position (like a serpent or "Kobra"). Light is emitted from tiny LEDs in the end so there is no need for a shade. It may not seem anything like an Anglepoise light, but just like Cawardine's lamp the form of Arad's PizzaKobra derives from its function and mechanism.

Function can affect not only the form of products like lamps, but even typefaces. In 1957, Swiss typographers Max Miedinger and Eduard Hoffmann designed Helvetica, a versatile font deliberately intended to be neutral. In the 2007 documentary film *Helvetica* by Gary Hustwit, the Dutch designer Wim Crouwel recalled: "Helvetica was a real step from the nineteenth-century typeface ....We were impressed by that because it was more neutral, and neutralism was a word that we loved. It should be neutral. It shouldn't have a meaning in itself. The meaning is in the content of the text and not in the typeface." This was in contrast with older fonts that may suggest classical or Gothic lettering, and hence symbolic or ethical values. In a sense, Helvetica sought to be ordinary and normal. Like good tools, we should be almost unaware of the font because its neutrality lets us see

BELOW:
No Angle, No Poise lamp
Designed by
Tiago da Fonseca,
UK, 2007

RIGHT:
PizzaKobra task light
Designed by Ron Arad,
Manufactured by iGuzzini,
Italy, 2007

Helvetica

Aa Ee Rr
Aa Ee Rr

Kunstgewerbeschule

abcdefghijklm
nopqrstuvwxyz
0123456789

only the message of the text it is communicating. It was designed in the period of high modernism when such functional neutrality was most celebrated: the same rational spirit can be seen in the electrical products designed by Dieter Rams for Braun around the same time.

Since the late 1980s the British designer Jasper Morrison has championed functionalist design principles. His early furniture and products were more like simplified illustrations than actual objects, and he pushed this point by producing stylized design drawings of his work. Morrison's style became known as "New Functionalism" in direct reference to the functionalist designs of the 1920s and 1930s, an association reinforced by their shared use of materials like plywood and tubular steel. It was as if Morrison was trying to design archetypal forms of objects; an ideal chair or a perfect bottle, for example. We might also see Helevetica as an archetypal letter form. Philosophically, the definition of archetypes relies on Plato's notion that ideal forms exist solely in the imagination, and actual objects can only imperfectly capture these ideals, like distorted reflections.

Morrison's interest in archetypes corresponded to his fascination with the normal, overlooked-but-perfect objects of everyday life, often anonymous designs that we simply take for granted: paper clips, kitchen appliances, wine glasses, combs, scissors and so on. In 2007 Morrison published a book with the Japanese designer Naoto Fukasawa about 204 examples of "super normal" objects, some by leading designers of their own generation, others anonymous examples of industrial design. Morrison became convinced that his own design should aspire as much as possible to be invisible, like the "super normal" designs he admired, because "There are better ways to design than putting a lot of effort into making something look special. Special is generally less useful than normal, and less rewarding in the long term. … The super normal object is the result of a long tradition of evolutionary

ABOVE:
Helvetica font
Designed by Max Miedinger
and Eduard Hoffmann,
Switzerland, 1957

advancement in the shape of everyday things, not attempting to break with the history of form but rather trying to summarise it." (jaspermorrison.com)

Industrial Facility is the name of the design partnership of husband-and-wife team Sam Hecht and Kim Colin. They design a range of industrially manufactured products, from furniture to home appliances such as clocks, steam cookers and torches, and to electronic devices such as telephones, projectors and computer hard drives. All their designs are informed by a single guiding idea: objects should be simple to understand and simple to use. A comparison of calculators designed by Industrial Facility and Naoto Fukasawa, both for Japanese clients, shows the similarity of their design philosophies. Both devices are undecorated monochrome plastic blocks. Industrial Facility's calculator has fewer keys but these are very prominent. Both calculators display up-to-date features: Industrial Facility's calculator plugs into a computer and Fukasawa's calculator has clever +Tax and −Tax buttons. The simplicity of these oblong designs owes much to Dieter Rams.

Industrial Facility could be said to be strict modernists adhering to the "form follows function" mantra, but there is more nuance than this. The designers want to draw attention to things that are generally overlooked by giving them a sense of presence and a distinctive appearance, but they are also concerned with allowing some products to blend into the fabric of our lives and spaces by giving them a quiet simplicity that does not jar visually. One example is a projector they designed that could be upended and shelved like a book when not in use. Sam Hecht elaborates on why simple forms are important: "The future will be simpler. It needs to be, if we are to continue to consume technology, where the illustration of complexity is of no importance, where only its results matter. Form will become mechanical, with its roots in the ordinary. As projects involve greater complexity, the more resonant their honesty needs to be."

BELOW LEFT:
Calculator M
Designed by Naoto Fukasawa,
Manufactured by Plus Minus
Zero Co. Ltd, Japan, 2008

BELOW RIGHT:
Ten Key calculator
Designed by
Industrial Facility,
Manufactured by IDEA
International, Japan, 2008

The Kindle e-reader was launched by online retailer Amazon in 2007 and is an example of how complex technology is hidden within a simple form for maximum clarity. The Kindle exploits innovative e-ink technology to digitally replicate the look of printed pages. Smaller than most paperbacks, the Kindle can store and access the content of many thousands of books. In keeping with Sam Hecht's words, the Kindle does not "illustrate complexity" and is deliberately very simple, keeping its technology well concealed. Like the Helvetica font, the Kindle's form does not get in the way of the words it shows us. It does not attempt to replicate the shape and form of a book, but instead every effort is made to simulate the feel of reading individual printed pages.

Sportswear brands frequently emphasize how their products can enhance performance, and the form of sports clothing often prioritizes function over appearance (though not always, as a closer examination of the design of training shoes later in this book will show, see Chapter 10). A sportsperson's performance may be improved by breathable fabrics or strong, light materials such as carbon fibre in the design of equipment. Or it can come from attention to the way in which the clothing will be worn, for example the Goggle jacket, originally designed by Massimo Osti for drivers in the 1988 Mille Miglia, an open road endurance race in Italy. In 2008 Aitor Throup was invited to update the jacket by the original manufacturer, fashion label C.P. Company. He recut the jacket around the shape of the human body in a driving position with arms bent and slightly forward, and excess volume in the back of the jacket for comfort, in what fashion critic Sarah Mower described as "ergonomically correct 'conceptual functionalism'".

Another jacket, this time designed by Will Carleysmith for the iconic British folding bicycle manufacturer Brompton, shares a similar approach to functional design. In looks the Oratory jacket is a classic and unremarkable example of traditional tailoring. But Carleysmith has designed it with features suitable for city cycling, such as underarm vents, special bamboo fabric lining to draw moisture away from the body, and an expandable concealed rear pleat borrowed from the design of shooting jackets that allows a forward leaning cycling posture. In addition, the jacket has reflective panels under the cuffs and collar, and another panel that can pull out on the back, to ensure a cyclist's safety. Here, the activity of cycling along with the necessity of keeping the same clothes on once you have arrived (at work, perhaps) have been combined in the brief, resulting in a purely functional garment that is nonetheless very far from the conventional fluorescent tabards or nylon anoraks designed for cyclists.

The ability of a designed object to function successfully is intimately related to the form its designer gives it, but unlike the dogmatic early modernists, today's designers see that there are numerous routes to achieve a successful marriage of form and function. As we have seen with the case of the Anglepoise lamp and its many successors, functional efficiency can be achieved in various ways, depending on the whim of the designer and the intended context for the product. The appearance of the product may also come down to the style choices of the designer, which is the subject of the next chapter.

ABOVE:
Kindle e-book reader
Designed and manufactured
by Amazon, USA, 2007

RIGHT:
Oratory jacket
Designed by Will Carleysmith,
Manufactured by Brompton
Bicycle Ltd, UK, 2011

4. STYLING

"Industrial art begins when the aesthetic judgment of a designer is employed to determine the character of a manufactured article."

John Gloag
Industrial Art Explained, 1934

In the previous chapter we discussed how the function of an object may determine what it looks like, a subject to which we will return later when we explore ergonomics in more detail (see Chapter 7). This chapter explores products from a different angle, considering how their appearances may be influenced by considerations other than functional efficiency. Perhaps because aesthetic opinions are so varied, individual and open to misunderstanding, the application of a particular style to a product's design can be divisive. We are in the realm of "styling", a term that has been used alongside "design" but has a chequered history and has often been thought of in derisory terms.

During the nineteenth century the aesthetic appearance of a product was determined quite late in the design process, once the form and function had been settled. Styling was seen only in regard to any decoration applied to the product. The Victorian painter and educator William Dyce understood the importance of getting the look of products right, and was aware that consumers were drawn first by the charm of products' appearances rather than their engineered functions: "Ornamental art is an ingredient necessary to the completeness of the results of mechanical skill … [because] … the love of ornament is a tendency of our being." Today we might interpret Dyce as meaning that the role of designers is somehow just to dress up the innovations of engineers to make them palatable. He wrote, "Mechanical contrivances are like skeletons without skin, like birds without feathers – pieces of organization, in short, without the ingredient which renders natural productions objects of pleasure to the senses." In other words, designers gave style and appeal to the works of engineers.

In the 1890s the Scottish architect and designer Charles Rennie Mackintosh – no stranger to extreme stylistic statements in his designs – wrote, "There is hope in honest error, none in the icy perfection of the mere stylist." He was suggesting it is better for a designer to experiment but sometimes fail, whereas giving style to perfect products is a shallow exercise, only about surface impressions and ultimately inconsequential. The role of the designer-as-stylist was being considered more skeptically. Shortly afterwards, in 1910, the Austrian architect Adolf Loos famously declared ornament to be a crime and decreed that progress could only be achieved by stripping decoration from functional objects. Self-conscious aesthetic pleasure in the decorative appearance of products began to be anathema to the modern movement, especially in advanced industrial design. Decoration, styling and unnecessary ornament became entangled in the public mind. From being a creative contribution to the success of design, styling had been demoted and ultimately rejected. Of course, modernist design had its own style but this often derived from celebrations of the materials and processes involved, for example bent tubular steel in furniture, rather than applied decoration. In the minds of designers, critics and the public, *styling* came to be downgraded to *decorating*.

Much later, in the 1980s, the great Italian designer Vico Magistretti thought again about the differences between our understanding of *design* and what we think of as *styling*. "Styling has always been thought of as useless decoration, superimposition, superficial alteration," he wrote, "while design meant the search for the essential, the unambiguous quality of the only form possible, as if it was wished to endow the design with some ethical value and styling with an aestheticizing value, to the clear detriment of the latter." Arguably, problem-solving functional considerations, without any aesthetic agenda, is *engineering*, whereas we usually expect a degree of styling in a product intended for a consumer market. Magistretti appears to agree with William Dyce: design and styling are complementary and while design sought clarity of function, styling "wraps that function in a cloak that essentially expressed qualities that are called 'style' and that are decisive in making the quality of the object recognizable."

So the aesthetic of a product – its style – has been seen at times to have almost moral bearing. Not only can designers make products distinctive from rivals, they can add symbolic or metaphoric qualities to them too, in a bid to increase their appeal. They can even make products look as if they embody certain values. In no area of design has styling been more potent than in the automobile industry.

In the late 1920s the chairman of General Motors, Alfred Sloan with the assistance of Harley Earl, the Head of Design and later Vice President of General Motors, had introduced the idea of planned obsolescence into car design by ensuring swift seasonal changes in the external shape of vehicles that required no improvements in engineering quality or mechanical functionality. Soon other manufacturing sectors followed the lead of the Detroit motor giants and instigated annual restyling of their product lines in order to boost consumption. In this sense styling only equated to fashion and taste. Certainly by the 1950s automotive styling had reached it apotheosis; quasi-funtional additions such as tail fins, spoilers and speed stripes drawn directly from popular science-fiction fantasies were added to models one year and removed from subsequent models the next.

RETRO CAR STYLING

Styling characteristics of period or vintage cars are sometimes revived in mass-produced models, precisely to differentiate them from their rivals. The Nissan Figaro, a small candy-coloured car launched in 1991, recalled a 1960s Datsun Fairlady but also looked consciously like a toy (readers of a certain age will see it as the toy car driven by children's book character Noddy). This styling was intentional: its looks let us know it is a plaything, not a utility or high-performance vehicle that we should take more seriously. More recently, the looks of the Chevrolet HHR (Heritage High Roof) and the Chrysler PT Cruiser suggested sedans from the film *Bugsy Malone* (1976), complete with running boards straight from the 1920s.

ABOVE:
Figaro
Manufactured by Nissan, Japan, 1991

LEFT:
Noddy
Children's book character created by
Enid Blyton, UK,
Published between 1949 and 1963;
TV series since 1955

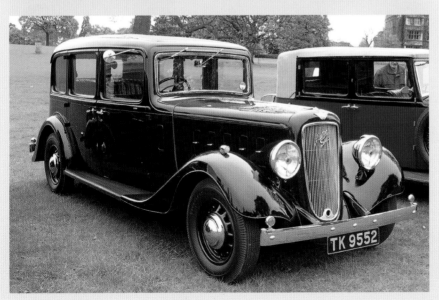

TOP:
HHR (Heritage High Roof)
Manufactured by Chevrolet, USA, 2006-11

MIDDLE:
PT Cruiser
Manufactured by Chrysler, USA, 2000-10

BOTTOM:
Austin Six
Austin Motor Company, 1931-37

Features like tail fins suggest that a car is more aerodynamic without really delivering any tangible mechanical or physical advantage; their nonetheless powerful appeal shows how the styling of a product calls on emotional responses other than pure logic. If we are led to think a car is faster because it has style elements borrowed from the popular imagination of space-ship design, we are inclined to think it is a better product than those without these features. In fact, mid-twentieth century "stretched" cars were gas-guzzling, weighty and inefficient. Although we now see them as deceptive, even wasteful, they are also acknowledged as iconic extremes of vehicle design, especially when compared to the rather bland, uniform, indistinguishable cars of today. Style, therefore, is very much "in the eye of the beholder" and can be read differently at various times, depending on the point of view and prevalent aesthetic of the age.

"Retro-styled" car design was popular in the 1990s, the period of late postmodernism where stylistic revivals, puns and references were fashionable and common in all design disciplines. This trend has abated, but nonetheless designers have not wholeheartedly re-embraced pure functionalist design. Styling is still prevalent where designers and manufacturers hope to make their products stand out from those of rivals that may perform in the same way, or where they want to imbue them with greater symbolic meaning. Styling can have emotional or nostalgic resonances for users, for example by reminding them of products from their youth. Often this may mean referring to historical styles, materials or proportions, or even to obsolete technologies, such as the range of retro telephone handsets manufactured by the small British firm Hulger that recall the clunky, heavy plastic handsets of 1960s and 1970s telephones. These are just the kinds of telephones that have been rendered entirely obsolete by mobile handsets and ironically the Hulger appliances are designed to plug into mobile telephones to

BELOW LEFT:
Hulger P*Phone, handset for mobile telephone
Manufactured by Hulger, UK, 2005

BELOW RIGHT:
Old School Dialler, mobile telephone app
Developed by Wagado, 2011

ABOVE:
**Plumen 002 low-energy
light bulb**
Designed by Bertrand Clerc,
Manufactured by Hulger,
UK, 2014

give users "authentic retro telephonic experiences". Perhaps even more ridiculous, because they seem utterly retrogressive and anti-intuitive, are the numerous applications for smart phones that simulate the experience of analogue telephone dials, or the addition of gratuitous "clicking shutters" to digital cameras in telephones (a kind of audio styling).

Hulger is also known for a radical redesign of the humble low-energy light bulb, the Plumen 001, designed by Samuel Wilkinson. The Plumen's design celebrates the luminescent core of the bulb by giving it an organic, sculptural shape that encourages us to leave it exposed rather than masking it behind a shade. The form also recalls the familiar globular or droplet shape of a conventional incandescent light bulb, almost as a graphic outline or representation rather than as a replica: we can say that it is styled to refer to a light bulb with which we are familiar and which many consumers were sad to see pass when it was phased out. This is a more sophisticated and accomplished styling exercise than the Hulger phones, which are really gimmicks and novelties because they are too literal.

But perhaps this is precisely Magistretti's point: the visual appearance – the styling – of a product's functional qualities is what gives it character and does not necessarily conceal its function behind decoration, and, as such, good styling adds to a product rather than detracting from it. This could be said of the Dualit toaster, which brought the industrial-chic styling of heavy-duty, commercial kitchen equipment into homes in the 1980s and 1990s. Arguably the opposite is true of the Juicy Salif lemon squeezer designed by Philippe Starck for the Italian manufacturer Alessi in 1990. On three long legs, and vaguely bullet-shaped, the squeezer's looks owed much to comic-book science-fiction rocket design, rather like Harley Earl's cars, and both are symbols of the conspicuous consumption that marked their eras. These are products styled primarily to catch the eye and send out messages about their owners' wealth, social rank and fashionable taste. Starck even declared that Juicy Salif was "not meant to squeeze lemons" but "to start conversations". It certainly failed to function anywhere near as well as the anonymous lemon squeezers commonly available at a fraction of the cost in kitchen equipment shops. For certain, Juicy Salif is not the only Alessi product with a proclaimed function that is quite secondary to its symbolic and decorative qualities, but its distinctive styling serves to distinguish it in a crowded market place and it has proved commercially very successful. In this sense, styling succeeds in adding considerable profit margins for designers and manufacturers.

BELOW:
NewGen toaster
Manufactured by Dualit, UK,
Late 1940s – present day

RIGHT:
Juicy Salif lemon squeezer
Designed by Philippe Starck
Manufactured by Alessi,
Italy, 1990

Some designers have built entire careers by formulating very distinctive signature styles, for example Spaniard Jaime Hayon, all of whose products and installations, from furniture to exhibition design, ceramics and lighting, relate to one another as parts of an imaginative fantasy world. Hayon frequently gives his designs loosely anthropomorphic characteristics, so they appear like cartoon characters capable of expressing emotion. His background as a decorator of skateboards gives his work a lively graphic quality. Hayon pays as much attention to the surface of his products as he does to their form and functionality: for him, conventional distinctions between design and styling are collapsed together. Much of Jaime Hayon's design output is for the mass market, albeit at the luxury end. But he also designs limited edition or unique products destined for the collectors' market through specialist galleries. Design for the gallery market often relies heavily on visual appearance to establish a designer's uniqueness. These works are frequently more symbolic and decorative than functional in a strict sense. They may purport to have uses – as vases, chairs, lamps, etc – but it is unlikely they will be used for these purposes very much, or at all, not least because of their expense. Here, the style of the product is intended to communicate the design philosophy of the designer, which may include a reverence (or irreverence) for materials and techniques, or extreme experiments with structure and purpose.

Right:
Mon Cirque installation
Designed by Jaime Hayon, 2006

CAPTION:
iMac personal computer
Manufactured by Apple, USA, 1998

However, most styling occurs with industrially made, mass-market products. Until the mid-1990s the styling of computers made by all manufacturers was generally similar: they were grey plastic boxes intended to be as neutral as possible in the corporate and office environments where most were located. As computer technology advanced and miniaturized, and computers themselves proliferated – especially after the establishment of the Internet – a startling transformation occurred, pioneered by Apple but widely copied. The Apple iMac, introduced in 1998, was as far from the usual grey box as it could be. The translucent, candy-coloured polycarbonate housings drew attention to the computer rather than encouraging it to blend in. The styling was the work of British-born designer Jonathan Ive, Senior Vice President of Design at Apple. The brave decision to radically restyle such an expensive product resoundingly transformed not only the market for computers but the fortunes of Apple too. Computers ceased to be nerdish office equipment and became lifestyle fashion accessories, bought by individuals as well as corporations for personal use in the home. The bright colours made iMacs approachable, even lovable, and the translucent casing let users glimpse the mysterious internals without having to worry about how they worked. It was essential that the products had distinctive style in order to place them apart from the grey boxes of rivals, which in comparison suddenly seemed old-fashioned and boring.

Decisions about the outward appearance of products will always be divisive because aesthetics and taste are personal, subjective opinions. Yet it is clear that the way a product looks can affect how consumers receive it. The car and clothing industries long ago accepted that seasonal adaptation of their products' appearances helps to stimulate market demand, so novelty, innovation and even fantasy inform how they look. In contrast, other products are designed to evoke history or archetypes, tapping into our common memory and desire for nostalgia.

5. UNIVERSALITY VERSUS INDIVIDUALISM

A at two extremes we can think of design as either an activity that affects as many people as possible by shaping products we all use, or as the personal and individual expression of a designer's ideas for their own benefit. Universal design solutions might seem totally at odds with an individualistic approach; the tension between design at a macro, global, scale and at a micro, local, scale is the subject of this chapter.

The structures of global trade and international manufacturing favour a "one-size-fits-all" approach to designing products. After all, it is most efficient and profitable to make countless multiples of a product that will appeal in numerous markets and be accessible to as many consumers as possible. Some products gain global status and can claim, in this sense, to be universal, usually because they are made by very rich and able manufacturers with ample budgets to ensure they can infiltrate all markets: Coca-Cola's ubiquity demonstrates this. The global availability of filter-tipped cigarettes in many regional varieties also shows how the tobacco industry succeeded with its products. Both examples are quickly consumed commodities that affect the body, and all products intended for personal comfort, grooming and well-being can naturally generate mass appeal, so that brands like Gillette and L'Oréal are global. Manufacturers of consumer technology products like telephones, cameras, televisions and stereo systems are necessarily large and complex businesses with great reach: Panasonic, Sony, Samsung and Philips products are recognizable everywhere. Similarly, the magnitude of the car industry makes Ford, Toyota and many other marques into global players. They all represent the apex of industrial design, creating complex products using the latest technological and material innovations, assembling vast quantities of products to

OPPOSITE & BELOW:
Sugru self-setting rubber
Invented by Jane Ní Dhulchaointigh,
Manufactured by Sugru,
UK, 2003

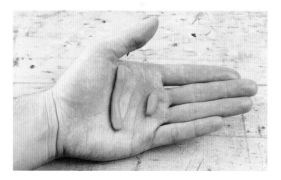

achieve cost efficiencies, and managing intricate supply and distribution systems.
Critics of globalism pick up on this, declaring that to find identical telephones,
razors, cars and other consumer goods in Alaska and Adelaide, New Delhi and
New York creates only a bland, placeless world. Small wonder, therefore, that many
designers remain perplexed about how they can possibly make an impact on these
behemoth systems, despite their willingness and expertise in designing for industry.
The systems are simply too big, too universal.

One approach is to match the enormous, macro-scale of industrial production
with a micro-scale attention to small details. Designers can interfere with the
ubiquity of mass-produced goods by customizing and individualizing them. This
is the purpose of Sugru, a synthetic compound invented and patented by Irish
designer Jane Ní Dhulchaointigh. In itself, Sugru is simply a soft paste that will
harden once it is exposed to air. It can become anything you want it to be, and its
purpose is to adapt existing products. For example, the owner of a camera can
reinforce it with Sugru to make it easier to hold (and safer to drop) when it is lent
to a child. Sugru can also fix broken products. Unlike the vast majority of products,
it does not have a single form or sole purpose and it is not complete until its user
has applied it. Sugru lets users customize and individualize standard products and
as such it is part of a trend towards hacking design that we shall explore in more
depth in Chapter 12.

ANTI-THEFT CAR / BIKE DEVICE

Dominic Wilcox often looks at the world ironically and designs products that are small, sometimes humorous interventions into existing systems. In 2008 he designed the Anti-theft Car/Bike Device that was, in truth, just a packet of stickers designed to look like damage to pristine paintwork. He commented:

"These rust and scratch stickers are designed to make your beautiful bike/car look rusted and scratched so that passing thieves assume it's not worth stealing due to its apparent shabbyness.

"Note. This anti-theft device is not guaranteed to work in any way. However I have stuck them to my shiney [sic] new red bike and can confirm it hasn't been stolen yet. 13 days of not being stolen in London probably equates to 7 years of non-stealing in the friendly countryside." (dominicwilcox.com)

With this very simple product Wilcox was able to comment upon the esteem we place on box-fresh new products versus used goods, and provide consumers with a way to customize their own products, with a vague sense that it may even have a beneficial result.

LEFT:
Anti-theft Car/Bike device
Designed by Dominic Wilcox,
UK, 2008

ABOVE:
Re-Done bicycle
Designed by Tristan Kopp,
The Netherlands, 2012

Both Sugru and Dominic Wilcox's stickers are adaptations that can be easily added to existing products. However, they can only make peripheral, if any, impact on industrial systems of production. Other designers have thought about how to intervene further into the design of products, perhaps by designing universal components that can be customized by individuals to suit their own purposes.

Bicycles are a major export product from Taiwan and are ridden all over the world. Even though the form of bicycles has been established for a century, manufacturers still make innovations, usually by introducing lighter and stronger materials, or by finding ways to simplify production and so lower costs. Yet it remains the case that the vast majority of bicycles are sold complete and ready to use. In contrast, Dutch designer Tristan Kopp rethought the product and divided it into components that can be easily sourced individually (for example, lengths of tubular steel, wheels and the saddle) and those more elaborate and specific connecting modules that would dictate the final form, which he designed himself. His Re-Done Bicycle is simply a set of connectors that cyclists can use as the framework for assembling their own bikes out of any materials they wish to use. It is a very personal riposte to the impersonal world of manufactured products, and introduces an element of craftsmanship into consumption. On the other hand, it would still require quite considerable skill to assemble a bike oneself, as well as access to numerous tools. And what is more, the bicycles that result may not be as comfortable, efficient or, crucially, as safe, as conventional manufactured bikes that have been tested and evaluated during the design and production processes. The spirit of this individualistic attitude to mass-production is laudable but it omits the benefits of large-scale industrial fabrication such as quality control, precision and complexity.

Wei Lun Tseng also thought about the components that make up products and how they might be customized. In this case, the products were domestic electrical goods like fans, lamps and kitchen appliances. He designed a set of universal modules that could be assembled in numerous configurations to create different products. In principle the project is very sensible, as it could reduce the quantities of products that are manufactured and even provide users with kits of components they could reconfigure for use as and when they were needed, therefore reducing the quantity of products consumed. But in reality, this speculative idea would require enormous research and development, and would be unlikely to yield satisfactory results. Multi-functional, flexible products, from Swiss army knives to sofa beds, seldom work as well as single-function specialist items. They may be made of similar materials but the functional requirements of an electric kettle are quite different to that of a fan or lamp, so in reality they are better designed individually. Arguably it may be possible to design components that are common to several products, but as the designer's prototypes show, this is too easily reduced to a simplistic family of geometric forms.

It is astounding that complicated electrical products such as kitchen appliances, with hundreds or even thousands of components and numerous materials, can be manufactured, shipped and retailed for profit for only a few pounds. The industrial and trade systems involved are necessarily vast and able to achieve economies of scale by automating processes and making large quantities of goods. Thomas Thwaites explored the system that makes it possible to manufacture and sell a domestic toaster for less than £4. To do so he set out to design and make his own toaster completely from scratch, including sourcing his own raw materials and creating his own tools that would replicate on an individual scale the processes of mass-manufacturing. Thwaites succeeded, just about. But his toaster could never look anything like a box-fresh, machine-made example, or function anywhere near as well. His odyssey used design thinking and problem solving as critical tools to unpack the often-concealed realities of the modern world, in this case the enormous amount of invention and consumption of resources that are expended to produce everyday household items. More than most designers, Thwaites managed to insert himself deep into the design and production systems of universal products to give his own very personal and individual interpretation.

In the design of furniture, one of the most radical and long-lasting innovations was the steam-bending of wooden components to industrially manufacture chairs, pioneered in the mid-nineteenth century by Michael Thonet. Prior to this, furniture was essentially handmade: Thonet enabled furniture to be mass-produced on a huge scale. He also effectively invented the idea of knock-down furniture, because he reconsidered the components, reducing the number of parts of an entire chair to just six pieces and 10 screws. Unassembled, 36 of these Model No. 14 chairs could be packed into one cubic metre, ensuring they were extraordinarily easy to distribute. Having designed the chairs in 1859, by 1891 Thonet had sold 7.3 million of them, surely qualifying it as a truly universal product.

Thonet industrialized chair production, but the process of steam-bending ash or beech wood is not in itself hugely technical and can be reduced to a small scale. This is what designer Joseph Pipal proposed in 2012 with his personal steam-bending factory. He designed a flexible jig that could be adapted to create a series of steam-bent forms, each of which could be used as parts of several different products from a child's toy bike to a chair. His intention was to miniaturize an industrial process to the scale of a single person, and to design a kit for all stages of production that could be easily transported and set up in temporary homes. He explained the project:

"My work focuses on the making process: tools, rigs and workshops that are socially minded and encourage engagement, understanding and participation. I am interested in how design navigates between utility and concept. A designer can be both the means of production (the making) and the model for production (the design), and therefore is well positioned to devise new concepts that challenge convention and offer alternatives to accepted models of production."

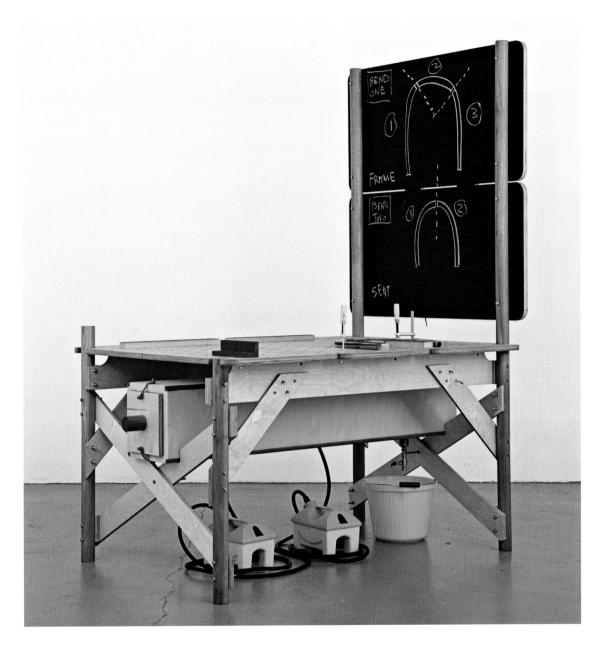

LEFT:
Child's bicycle
Designed and made by Joseph Pipal using the
Sweatshop portable steam-bending bench,
UK, 2012

ABOVE:
Sweatshop portable steam-bending bench
Designed and made by Joseph Pipal, UK, 2012

Today, most of us have no idea how products are made, and care even less. The products themselves seldom reveal their secrets either, being designed in such a way as to conceal traces of production processes. By revealing how steam bending is done, Pipal demystified it, re-engaging us with the ways in which our products are made. He also wanted to personalize and individualize the process: it would be possible to order single bespoke products from his factory in a way that would be impossible at Thonet's. Pipal's miniature factory reduces a global industry to a scale suitable for local production, and he believes that it has potential social as well as practical benefits. In a sense he is echoing William Morris and others whose Arts and Crafts movement sought to dignify the labour of artisans and makers. A similar spirit exists in Will Shannon's Cabinet Maker project, for which he designed a mobile factory mounted on a bicycle. His intention was to collect discarded materials, such as waste timber, old newspapers and detritus like broken suitcases, from the streets around his Hackney home and use them to make new furniture. Like Pipal, Shannon's design process had a social and economic agenda:

"My ambition is to develop an informal factory whose disparate employees – professionals as well as enthusiastic amateurs – are spread throughout the city, at work in their own cabinet making production facilities: turning wood in the shed in Bermondsey, or making papier mâché in Dalston."

Perhaps both Pipal and Shannon are really looking at designing as a means of empowerment. In truth, neither of their projects would make the slightest impact on established manufacturing methods but they do draw our attention to them, and give their participants more control over the shaping of the world. The notion of empowerment suggests a greater degree of ownership and command; consumers feel empowered when they are permitted to customize the products they use. For this reason, numerous products are designed to be customized, even in very small ways, to help their manufacturers connect more fully with consumers (and, of course, gain and retain their custom). Buyers of new cars, for example, can specify paint finishes, upholstery and extras from a predetermined list of choices. For the comfort and safety of drivers, car seats are adjustable to suit most body shapes and sizes. The appearance of computer and telephone screens can be altered and individualized by users, as can their external cases. In a sense, the "one-size-fits-all" philosophy of universal-scale mass production has evolved from Henry Ford's much quoted adage that a customer could choose any colour for one of his cars as long as it was black, to a situation where a company like Apple supplies neutral products that are not really completed until they have been customized by their eventual users. Seen like this, we can think of the mighty Apple Inc. in the same way as humble Sugru: both make products that are only finished once they are in your hands.

RIGHT:
Metro Cabinet
Designed and made by
Will Shannon, UK, 2011

UNIVERSALITY VERSUS INDIVIDUALISM

6. MATERIALS & TECHNOLOGIES

To make a chocolate teapot would be an absurd joke because it could not work: chocolate melts. This idea emphasizes the important relationship between materials and design. All tangible products are made of something, and often they are made of combinations of materials each selected for their particular qualities. The head of a hammer, for example, is made of steel because aluminium would be too soft and too light for the job. Hard, heavy steel gives the hammer force. The handle, however, can be lighter so wood is often used. In combination, the wood and steel unbalance the hammer, which in this case is a positive attribute because the choice of unequally weighted materials enhances momentum when the hammer is used, making the head more powerful on impact. But perhaps the smooth wooden surface of the handle is difficult to grasp, so many hammers have coatings or textured grips made of rubber or a synthetic material. The steel, wood and rubber all have inherent properties and a designer's task is to find the most appropriate materials to meet the brief.

In this chapter we will explore the main groups of materials used for industrial design. This cannot be exhaustive as the world of material science is both very established and very varied. Special emphasis will be given to new material experiments and their potential to transform design. We will also touch upon the technologies that have been developed to process materials but, once again, the history of manufacturing techniques is very long and complex so we will focus on new and emerging techniques. Some materials, such as silk or precious metals, were so valued and became such powerful cultural forces that empires were built upon their trade. Even today, international trade in raw materials shapes global economies.

Many designers create material libraries or archives of samples from manufacturers, off-cuts, salvaged fragments, or collections of products and objects that are made in similar ways that may be inspirational. In doing this they learn about the strengths and weaknesses of common materials and can make informed judgments about when best to use them. All designers need to be in command of the materials most closely associated with their discipline: cutlery designers need first and foremost to know about metal and fashion designers must understand textiles, for example.

Only once designers have a thorough knowledge of their materials, and the techniques that have been invented for handling them, can they begin to "break the rules" and explore new uses for materials and techniques. These experiments are often the most absorbing and fruitful design activities because they contain great potential for exciting new discoveries, as well as risks of failure. Since solving problems lies at the heart of design, it is little surprise that many designers enjoy applying design thinking to reimagine their materials.

Scientists may be more likely than designers to invent entirely new materials, such as Graphene, a honeycomb lattice of carbon just one atom thick. Graphene is one of the thinnest materials in the world, and also one of the strongest and hardest. Its invention won Nobel prizes in 2010 for two Russian-born physicists at Manchester University, Andre Geim and Konstantin Novoselov. Graphene is also almost transparent and conducts heat and electricity better than most other materials. Clearly its potential to transform industrially-made products is enormous. Designers welcome scientific innovations such as Graphene because they have the skills to give shape and purpose to materials. Progress in the development of plastics has frequently been driven by innovations in industry, such as the invention of polypropylene by the Italian chemist Giulio Natta in 1954. Polypropylene was manufactured by Shell and in 1963 Robin Day won a design competition sponsored by the company to promote the material. Day's Polyprop chair became one of the most successful British designs of the decade. A similar story lies behind the development of Konstantin Grcic's MYTO chair, discussed in Chapter 1.

Designers need not rely on the innovations of scientists but can explore materials themselves. The natural world is full of materials that we have only just begun to understand and exploit. For example, the fast-growing luffa plant is grown only for its large seedpods that are dried and used as scrubbers for bathing. But Mauricio Affonso explored luffa and discovered how it could be used to make a paper-like material suitable for air filters, and that it could be easily and cheaply moulded. It has antibacterial qualities and is breathable, making it excellent for medical applications, so he designed splints for wrist injuries made of moulded luffa. He even conceived giant nets of luffa that could be used for capturing

BELOW LEFT:
Dr Rahul R. Nair with a sample of one micron thick Graphene oxide film

BELOW RIGHT:
Luffa medical splints
Designed by Mauricio Affonso, UK, 2013

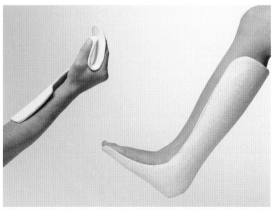

LEFT:
Venus Natural Crystal chair
Designed by Tokujin Yoshioka,
Japan, 2008

RIGHT:
1.3 chair
Designed by Kihyun Kim,
UK, 2012

pollution, such as chemical leaks or oil spills, because it is so absorbent. Affonso did not limit his design brief in any way, but systematically explored the enormous potential of a material that, until now, had been largely overlooked.

Japanese designer Tokujin Yoshioka has gone a step further by encouraging crystals to grow around a mesh framework to create a crystal chair. Here, our sense of order and logic (perhaps symbolized by mass-production of identical units in factories) is in tension with the order and logic of natural patterns.

WOOD AND PAPER

Timber has been a traditional material for architecture, furniture, tools and household implements worldwide for millennia because of its availability and the relative ease of processing. The strength, size and density of trees varies greatly from species to species and each type of wood has been exploited differently depending on its qualities. Oak's large scale and strength suited it to the frames of buildings and ships, while narrow but dense and hard boxwood logs were ideal as printing blocks for wood engravers because the timber could be polished very smooth and would receive fine engraved details. At the opposite extreme, balsa is fast-growing, extremely soft and lightweight. It grows in the American tropics where it was used to build rafts; today it is mostly a model-making material.

Craftsmen working solid wood have developed a broad range of carpentry and cabinet-making skills, equipment and conventions, responding to the character of raw timber. For example, traditional techniques like mortise and tenon or dovetail joints rely on the natural shrinkage of wood as it dries to secure the connections. From the eighteenth century onwards, industrial processes began to replace hand skills thus enabling increased standardization of wood products: for example, mechanical saws ensure even planks and drying kilns speed up the seasoning of green wood. Perhaps the greatest innovations were laminating techniques that bonded very thin sheets of wood together in layers in which the wood grain was opposed, creating what we now know as plywood. Plywood can be moulded and cut in ways that are impossible with solid timber and rapidly it became a staple material of the furniture industry. Another industrial innovation was steam-bending to shape timber (see Chapter 5).

The principle areas of research and development of wood today are around issues of sustainability. The management of natural as well as farmed forestry resources has become a major concern because of unregulated logging. Designers and manufacturers are increasingly aware they must only use timber from

accredited sustainable sources. Innovative designers are also maximizing timber resources by finding ways to use wood waste, clever processes to use less timber, or surprising uses of unfamiliar woods. For example, South Korean designer Kihyun Kim designed a chair made of balsa wood weighing only 1.28kg. Balsa may be light but it is not strong, so Kim compressed it into hardwood veneer shells to make the chair's components. The shells act as a kind of exoskeleton shielding the balsa inside.

Fellow countryman Seongyong Lee was inspired by the way cardboard tubes are made when he invented Plytube, a revolutionary wooden tube system constructed of rolled veneers. Although he initially made prototypes by hand, the system is eminently appropriate for industrial mass-manufacture. The tubes are strong, lightweight and smooth to touch, and have potential for furniture and architectural applications.

The desire to make more with less timber was also Benjamin Hubert's intention for the Ripple table. It has a patented corrugated plywood construction that gives it a high strength-to-weight ratio and, weighing in at only 12.5kg, the designer claims Ripple uses 80 per cent less wood than solid timber tables.

ABOVE:
Plytube stools
Designed by Seongyong Lee, UK, 2010

ABOVE RIGHT:
Ripple Table 2.0
Designed by Benjamin Hubert, UK, 2014

BELOW RIGHT:
Detail of the Ripple table's structure

Both Hubert and Lee explored wood's flexibility and this has also been exploited with Bendywood®, an innovative wood product manufactured by Candidus Prugger in Italy. European beech has the optimum cell structure to allow planks to be compressed by 20 per cent along their length while damp. Once dry, the wood can be bent to a radius 10 times its thickness (for example a 25mm board can be bent to a radius of 250mm). Initially marketed to make mouldings for furniture, kitchen cabinets or interior architecture, the applications for Bendywood are limitless as it retains all the characters of untreated wood with the added benefit of extreme flexibility.

These innovative uses of processed timber decrease weight without compromising strength, meaning timber supplies can go further. Dutch designer Marjan van Aubel, together with James Shaw, had similar intentions but chose a more radical direction. They mixed sawdust with bio-resin to produce the Well Proven chair. Sawdust reacts with the bio-resin by expanding to five times its previous volume before setting hard. Through this process the designers were able to make moulded wooden seat shells, a comfortable chair form but one that is generally made only with oil-based plastics. The designers set out to use sawdust that is produced as a waste product from wood processing. The quantity

ABOVE:
Bendywood®
Manufactured by
Candidus Prugger,
Italy, 2008

of sawdust that represents the amount of wood needed for one conventional chair could make five Well Proven chairs. While the Well Proven chair is made of a wood pulp, other designers have experimented with paper pulp as a structural material, for example Nacho Carbonell. His Evolution series of chairs are extreme forms, made as one-offs with pod-like papier mâché cocoons. They are made for a small market of collectors, but paper pulp is also a ubiquitous low-cost material widely used in packaging. A group of student designers at the Royal College of Art, Thomas Gottelier, Edward Thomas and Bobby Petersen, conceived a disposable bicycle helmet to be made of recycled newspapers and intended to be given away free to users of London's bicycle hire scheme. Here, an existing paper technology has been re-appropriated for an entirely new context.

The bicycle-helmet designers' brief set them the challenge to find a cost effective yet strong material to use for a disposable free giveaway. Their choice of paper pulp was also triggered by the context of their helmet; London's commuters discard millions of newspapers every day. By repurposing existing technology for recycling paper into packaging, they were proposing a closed circuit of production, consumption and disposal, since the helmets themselves were also recyclable. As with the Well Proven chair, this kind of design thinking addresses the total lifecycle of materials and products, and will be discussed in Chapter 12. French designer Ariane Prin was also considering product lifecycles when she designed a device to make pencils from reconstituted wood waste and discarded pigments from the studios and workshops of the Royal College of Art. In her hands, ubiquitous

ABOVE:
Evolution bench
Designed and made
by Nacho Carbonell,
The Netherlands, 2008

OPPOSITE:
Well Proven chairs
Designed by Marjan van
Aubel and James Shaw,
UK, 2012

wooden pencils became individually expressive and hand-crafted, in contrast to the industrially uniform pencils with which we are familiar.

The global market for furniture, and the environmental challenge posed by forestry to meet demand, has encouraged designers and manufacturers to look at alternatives to wood; one such is bamboo. A member of the grass family, bamboo is one of the fastest growing plants in the world and has many similar qualities to wood. It can be processed into very hard-wearing boards, rather like plywood in appearance, suitable for flooring or furniture. Israeli designer Jair Straschnow designed a range of flat-pack, self-assembly bamboo board furniture, including tables and shelf systems, entirely made of bamboo sheet laminates. He avoided glue and screws, preferring to adapt traditional dovetail joints and exploit the material's natural springiness to hold the structures in tension. He made the furniture prototypes himself, but large-scale commercial manufacturers, including Finland's Artek, have introduced mass-produced processed bamboo furniture.

Light and soft, cork is in fact the bark of the cork oak tree. The trend towards synthetic wine-bottle stoppers and screw tops has damaged the cork industry. Yet cork is a highly versatile and sustainable material that is pleasant to touch and has excellent insulation qualities. It can be milled and carved like wood, and reconstituted into boards or blocks. Designers are finding applications for it as shoe soles, bicycle saddles, insulation panels and domestic products such as lampshades.

CERAMICS AND GLASS

It is remarkable to think that our ancient forebears would recognize some of our everyday items because they too were familiar with ceramics and glass. The term "ceramic" was coined in the nineteenth century to encompass all forms of pottery and porcelain. Pottery is one of the oldest technologies in existence and also one of the most widespread because the clays from which pottery is made are widely dispersed. The more refined clays used for porcelain are rarer. Because of the fragility of the material, ceramic wares only replaced older techniques like basketry once people began to settle into communities in the middle Neolithic period, about 7,000 years ago. In the form of bricks or terracotta, ceramics have been staple construction materials shaping our built environment for thousands of years.

Put simply, ceramics are "fired earth": clay that has been heated in a kiln to dry and consolidate it. Since its invention, the material, technology and applications for ceramics may have been refined, but the principle remains unchanged. Ceramics played a pivotal role in the transformation from craft production to mass production during the Industrial Revolution when eighteenth-century entrepreneurs like Josiah Wedgwood succeeded in industrializing the manufacture of earthenware. Today, we are very familiar with ceramic tableware, sanitaryware and architectural details like tiles and mouldings. But new applications are being developed for ceramics: for example, foams. One method is to impregnate a material like expanded foam sponge with ceramic slurry prior to firing: in the kiln the sponge burns away leaving only the ceramic held in a cellular structure. By its nature this is much lighter by volume than solid ceramic. It is used primarily for heat or sound insulation products, but Marcel Wanders celebrated it as a consumer product for the home with his Sponge vase, designed in 1997. Dutch designer Marjan van Aubel has developed her own foamed porcelain that expands in the kiln rather like bread in an oven. Still only at prototype stage, the porcelain promises to be a way of making lightweight china that uses only a third of the material required for conventional ceramics. The cellular structure of foamed porcelain also makes the material very strong. In her early prototypes she explored the boundary of controlling the material with moulds and allowing it to behave freely, with some startling results.

We can think of cement as a ceramic on an architectural or engineering scale: like conventional ceramics, cements and concretes begin as liquid slurry but harden as they dry. The difference is that they do not need to be placed inside a kiln to cure the material. We often associate concrete with twentieth-century International Style architecture but the Romans perfected it 2,000 years ago. Foamed concretes have been developed that reduce the weight of buildings as well as the quantity of concrete required to build them. Since the construction industry is regarded as one of the most polluting, innovations that reduce the environmental impact of new buildings are to be welcomed. On a different note, the architecture firm Herzog & de Meuron used concrete decoratively, by etching photographs by Thomas Ruff over the entire façade of the Eberswalde Library, a building they completed in 1999.

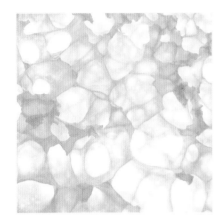

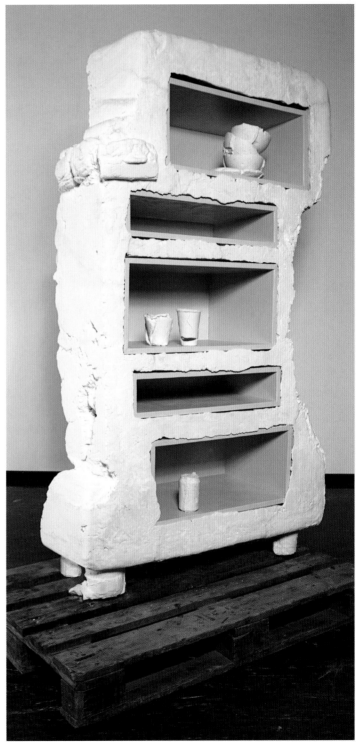

ABOVE & RIGHT:
Foam China shelving unit and detail
Designed by Marjan van Aubel,
Developed at the European Ceramic Work
Centre (EKWC), The Netherlands, 2009

NEW CERAMICS

Kyocera was formed in Kyoto in 1959 and today is the world's leading manufacturer of fine ceramics used by industry. These are remarkable high-performance materials that invisibly shape our world, at the intersection of science, engineering and design. Like diamond, Zirconia is extremely strong and tough, and it can be machined very precisely to make accurate components for medical equipment such as liquid drug delivery systems. It can be honed to a very sharp and fine cutting edge, so cutters and blades for industrial machinery are made of Zirconia. It also finds applications in electrical insulation and for precision parts of hard disk drive heads. Like a very advanced plastic, it can be extruded and pressed into extremely intricate components for complex machines.

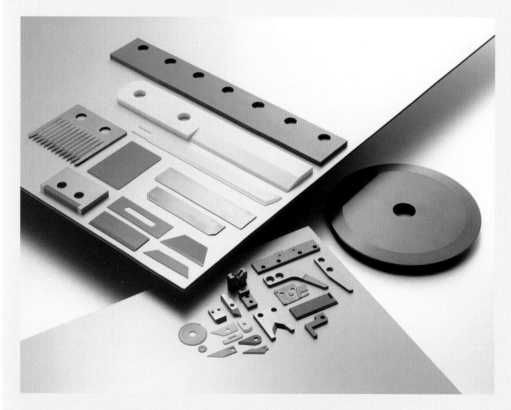

ABOVE:
Cutters and wear-resistant parts made of Zirconia
Manufactured by Kyocera, Japan

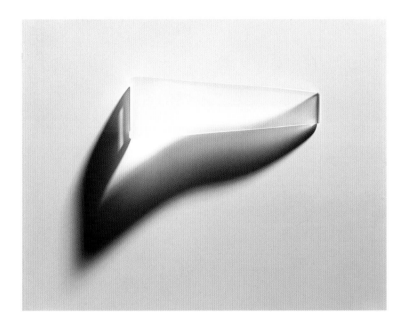

Razors are frequently made of plastic with steel blades and are not intended to last very long: after several uses the blade is blunt. This is extremely wasteful as they are disposed of when only one small part of the product has failed (an issue examined in much greater depth in Chapters 9 and 12). As long ago as 1991, Ross Lovegrove proposed a razor with a long-lasting Zirconia ceramic blade that would last for at least 150 shaves. Unfortunately it never reached production and a quarter of a century later disposable razors still dominate the market.

Glass is often thought of in tandem with ceramics because both processes use extreme heat to produce hard, brittle results from natural materials. In the case of glass, high temperatures fuse silica, usually derived from sand, flint or quartz, with the aid of an alkaline flux such as potash or soda. In its molten state glass is extremely malleable and can be moulded, blown or stretched. Unlike ceramics, glass can be recycled by simply breaking it up and melting the shards once again. It is thought glass was invented in the eastern Mediterranean about 2500 BC and Ancient Egyptian glass artifacts survive. Certainly sand, a source of silica, is very prevalent in the Sahara region. In 2010 Markus Kayser explored how sand could be transformed directly into a kind of 3D-printed glass just by focusing the sun's power on to it. His project, SolarSinter, is one of the most radical reinventions of glass-making in recent years. He explored it at a small scale, but his project was proof of principle that two seemingly endless natural resources – sunlight and desert sand – could be brought together as a fabrication method with no other environmental impact, such as pollution or the need for fossil fuels. It is not difficult to imagine huge mobile sintering machines traversing the desert expanses, sintering smooth glass roads as they progress!

ABOVE:
Razor with ceramic blade
Designed by Ross Lovegrove,
UK, 1991

ABOVE:
SolarSinter bowl
Designed and made by
Markus Kayser, UK, 2010

LEFT:
SolarSinter machine
Designed and made by
Markus Kayser, UK, 2010

ABOVE RIGHT:
**Soma light installation,
detail**
Designed and made by
Ayala Serfaty, Israel, 2008

RIGHT:
Glass chair
Designed by Thomas
Heatherwick and made by
Salviati, Italy, 2004

Murano, a series of islands in the Venetian Lagoon in north-east Italy, is famed for its glassmakers and many designers have worked with well-established firms such as Venini and Salviati because of their skill and craftsmanship. Thomas Heatherwick, ever the maverick designer, explored the potential of blown glass to be a structural material and with craftsmen at Salviati he developed a chair made entirely of three huge conjoined glass bubbles. On another occasion he proposed a glass bridge over a canal in north London. Glass has very high compressive strength (meaning it is strong when it is pressed) so Heatherwick proposed to make the bridge by pressing together over one thousand sheets of glass without any fixings, using gravity as the only force to maintain the structure. He proved the principle of his daring scheme with prototypes but the finished bridge was never built.

Designers are often drawn to hand-making processes such as mouth-blown glass because there is beauty in the irregularities that naturally appear. They ensure each piece is unique and can give the glassware an organic, natural character at odds with machine-made uniformity. The American glassmaker Dale Chihuly is probably the most successful and well-known studio glassmaker today, producing enormous configurations of glass that often evoke the shapes and colours of coral reefs. Israeli designer Ayala Serfaty has created extremely organic light installations built of intertwining forms of 2mm-wide glass filaments that she encases in a polymer membrane. They too have a delicacy that evokes the structure of coral.

METAL

Numerous metallic elements fill the periodic table and can be found within the geology of the planet. Metals have a special place in the development of human civilization and people first extracted iron by smelting ore 5,000 years ago, initially to make utensils and weapons. Bronze, an alloy composed of copper and tin but stronger than either alone, was developed about 3,000 years ago and gave its name to an entire era of social development: the Bronze Age. Metal implements, therefore, gave people advantages over both their rivals and their environmental conditions.

Over the millennia the techniques of handling metal were refined to become extremely sophisticated, and different metals or their compounds or alloys have been developed to suit many scales and purposes, from intricate jewellery made of precious metals to monumental structural engineering projects such as bridges or container ships. Metals are handled by individual craftsmen but also fabricated with massive industrial processes such as rolling, which transforms metal bars into sheets of even thickness. In this section we will explore how metals are used in contemporary design and some of the techniques used to handle them.

The earliest way for smiths to handle iron at their forges was to beat molten metal into shape while it was still hot and malleable (meaning it can be shaped by compression). Wrought iron can be worked into intricate forms and, until casting superseded it in the early nineteenth century, was popular for architectural details like balconies, lanterns and hinges. Wrought iron is still forged as it has always been and remains a popular technique amongst craftsmen to make durable items, for example Albert Paley, one of the best-known art-metalworkers today.

Casting molten metal in clay or sand moulds allowed metalworkers more refinement with their materials than forging, enabling them to create vessels, armour and other complex forms. Today cast-metal components are industrially produced, for example plumbing parts such as taps. When casts are first extracted from their moulds, it is possible to see how the molten metal has flowed into and through it. These additional spurs of metal are removed but can be easily recycled simply by throwing them back into the crucible. The designer Max Lamb was frustrated at his inability to access the facilities of a foundry, so he made his own sand-cast pewter furniture on beaches in Cornwall at low tide. The process was improvised but in principle identical to industrial techniques.

In contrast to Max Lamb's individual appropriation of casting techniques is metal injection moulding (MIM). Developed from the 1970s, it is a technique that treats metal like plastic. Finely powdered metal is mixed with a binder material to create a "feedstock" that can be handled by an injection-moulding machine. The material can be injected into very precise, detailed moulds to create durable components with very accurate dimensional tolerances that are suitable for medical, aerospace, automotive and military applications.

ABOVE:
Nebuli candleholders
Designed and made by
Albert Paley, USA, 2014

ABOVE:
Production casting and finished Axor tap
Designed by Antonio Citterio,
Manufactured by Hansgrohe, Germany, 2003

MAGNETISM

Magnetism is a strange, invisible natural force with origins in electrical currents and the attraction of elemental particles to one another. Some materials, including aluminium and plastic, have no magnetic fields: others, notably iron and its derivatives, are very magnetic.

Designers have exploited magnetism in different ways as active agents in their design processes. Tord Boontje introduced magnetic particles into resin and was able to control the holographic effect they produce by aligning the particles with an electrical current. It is a new type of surface finish that could be applied to many different products, from furniture to vehicles or fashion accessories.

RIGHT:
Magnetic Fields table
Designed and made by Tord Boontje, UK, 2013

Jólan van der Wiel harnessed magnetism and gravity to invent an entirely new manufacturing process that is the reverse of conventional moulding techniques. Rather than injecting or pouring molten metal into a mould to cast it, he magnetized resin and drew out the form of a stool by pulling the material with magnets. The spiky result expresses and captures the magnetic fields that are normally invisible.

ABOVE:
Gravity stool and the machine to make it
Designed and made by Jólan van der Wiel, The Netherlands, 2012

Extrusion is the method of forming a continuous cross-sectional profile by pushing malleable material through a shaped die, and is common in the production of plastic and metal products. As aluminium is a relatively soft metal, it lends itself to extrusion. Many diverse profiles of extruded aluminium exist and they are often used for lightweight frame structures, window frames and trims. Thomas Heatherwick discovered an extruding machine in the Far East capable of exerting 10,000 tonnes of pressure, designed to make parts for the aerospace industry, and of sufficient scale to fabricate an entire potentially endless extruded bench. The advantage of the process is that the metal profile is entirely consistent and even along its length, although as the process begins the metal is liable to contort until the flow evens out. Heatherwick liked these mutated areas best and left them attached to his benches.

ABOVE & LEFT:
Extrusion bench and extruding machine
Designed by Thomas Heatherwick, UK, 2009

In contrast to the metalworking processes described so far, which have been largely formative, moulding techniques, milling is a reductive process that removes material from a large mass to create the finished product. It is widely used in metalworking to fabricate precision components such as gears, but it is slower than casting processes. The milling tool is equipped with many cutting edges that each bite away tiny quantities of the metal, known as swarf, as they pass over it. Aluminium is one of the most popular choices of metal for product design because it is lightweight and plentiful. While milling is often a process to make hidden components of machinery, one well-known consumer product celebrates the technique by featuring milled aluminium prominently as its exterior casing: Apple's MacBook Pro laptop computer. The aluminium housing is stronger than plastic equivalents but light and seamless, with the additional advantage that it patinates with age and handling and does not require a paint finish.

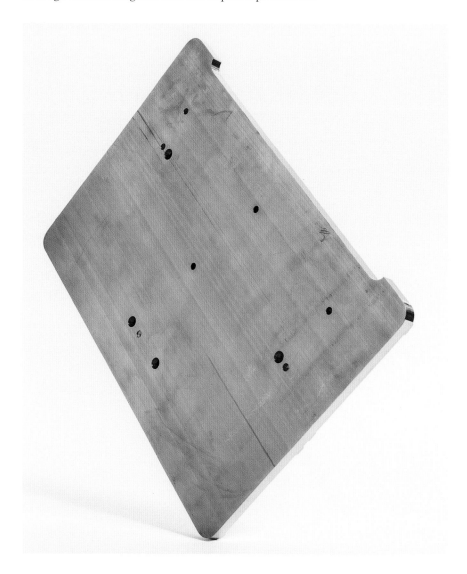

LEFT:
Macbook Pro laptop computer casing during production
Manufactured by Apple Inc,
USA, 2008

RIGHT:
Foliate ring
Designed by Ross Lovegrove,
UK, 2013

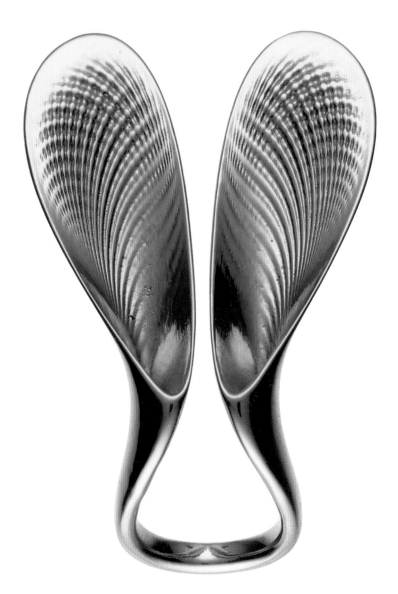

Metal spinning is a process akin to turning wood on a lathe. Flat discs or tubes of metal are rotated at high speed and pressed against a shaping block to create forms that are axially symmetrical, such as light fittings, gas cylinders, urns and even the nose cones of rockets. It is suitable for ductile metals that can be shaped under tensile stress, including stainless steel and aluminium.

The final metalworking process to consider is an additive technique still in its infancy: 3D printing. Chapter 8 will discuss 3D printing and other digital techniques in much more depth, but it is important to mention it in the context of working with metal as it provides designers and manufacturers with an entirely new way to give shape to metal. Only recently have machines been developed capable of printing with metals, and Ross Lovegrove has designed a collection of organically inspired rings printed in 18-carat gold to explore their potential.

PLASTIC

If there was to be a single material that came to define the twentieth century, it must be plastic in all its numerous guises, from buttons to cameras, inflatable chairs and sandwich wrappers. The term "plastic" derives from the Greek word *plastikos*, meaning to mould or shape. Today, the most remarkable quality of plastic is that there will be a type suitable for any shape, density, strength, flexibility or heat conditions. Plastics give form to the fruits of our imaginations and as such have had a profound effect on the way we experience the world, but we must ask whether they will shape the next century in the same way they formed the last.

Plastics are sometimes known as polymers as they all consist of long chains of hydrocarbon molecules. These occur in nature, for example in horn and shell or in our own fingernails and hair. We have found ways to extract plastics from animal and plant materials, such as casein which derives from milk, but most plastics are synthesized from fossil fuels: oil and coal. The plastic industry as we recognize it today began in 1844 when Charles Goodyear patented a process to stabilize natural rubber by mixing it with sulphur and curing it with heat and pressure, a method he called "vulcanization". By the early twentieth century numerous new plastics had been developed and patented, for example Bakelite, Catalin and Celluloid. These were used to mould products like inexpensive boxes, handles and dress accessories that previously were made of more costly natural materials such as mother-of-pearl, horn and ivory: very early on plastics became associated with simulation and low-cost mass production.

ABOVE:
Ty Nant water bottle
Designed by Ross Lovegrove,
UK, 2000-2002

The golden era for plastics coincided with the first wave of mass electrification between the world wars, and plastics were commonly used to make all manner of new electric consumer products, from radios to hairdryers, kitchenware to fans. By the middle of the twentieth century, plastic was the medium of choice for the burgeoning telecommunications industry, not only to make telephone handsets but for the infrastructure of the network itself, such as cable insulation. Just as much as it appealed to manufacturers of consumer goods, so plastics were developed for all manner of industrial and military applications too. In its lowliest form plastic packaging revolutionized the food industry and in its most sophisticated guises plastics enabled the space race and medical advances. Malleable plastic could become whatever we wanted it to be, and could be cast into any shape or size. By 1972 it was everywhere, leading the philosopher Roland Barthes to declare plastic to be "ubiquity made visible … less a thing than a trace of a movement". Ross Lovegrove's water bottle for Ty Nant perfectly captures what Barthes meant. We do not see the plastic, we see the water it contains as if frozen as it flows.

Because most plastics come from fossil fuels, we face the challenge of finite and fast-declining oil reserves. Today, the most exhaustive research is into bio-resins and other substitutes for oil-based compounds. Designers and manufacturers are looking at alternative or hybrid materials that have similar properties to plastics and can be substituted for them. Still, we have yet to abandon our love affair with oil-based products so it is beholden on designers to consider how to use them most responsibly, for example by ensuring components made of different plastics can be easily separated for recycling, or to use them

PLASTIC TYPES

Types of plastic can be divided into three groups, each with their own character.

Thermoplastics

Thermoplastics can be repeatedly reheated and remoulded, for example Polypropylene, a widely used material most commonly employed in high-volume, low-cost items like bottle tops or food containers. Polypropylene is strong yet flexible and was the perfect material for Robin Day's iconic 1960s Polyprop chair. It is also used to make rope and even carpets. Polyethylene is cheap and durable and is widely used for carrier bags and pipes. Tom Dixon used it to make his Jack lights by rotation moulding. A great advantage of many thermoplastics is that they can be endlessly recycled.

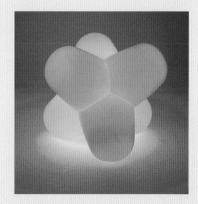

Thermosets

Unlike thermoplastics, the molecules of thermoset polymers are transformed when they are heated, making them permanently rigid and therefore impossible to recycle. Early twentieth-century phenolic plastics were a group of phenol-formaldehydes best known under the trade name Bakelite: products like ashtrays and radios were hard, brittle and opaque. Today heat- and electrical-resistant phenolics are still used for electrical plugs and circuitry, and lamp holders. Other widely used thermoset plastics are glass-reinforced plastic (GRP, also known as fibreglass) and silicones.

ABOVE:
Jack Light
Designed and made by
Tom Dixon, UK, 1996

LEFT:
MU folding plug
Designed by Min Kyu Choi,
Manufactured by
Made in Mind Ltd,
UK, 2009

Elastomers

Elastomers are thermoplastic or thermosetting polymers that have an inherent elasticity that allows them to retain their original shape after they have been distorted through pressure. We often think of elastomers collectively as rubber, although there are very many variants, some deriving from natural rubber and others synthetically produced. Elastomers are generally used where flexibility is key: for the soles of shoes, for example, or to make sealants.

more sparingly. Chemical giants, like BASF, that develop new plastics must continue to improve the ecological footprint of their products. Designers can help to change consumers' attitudes towards plastics by designing products with more innate and lasting value, in order to defeat our expectation that plastics, although ubiquitous, are ephemeral and disposable.

The desire to revalue plastic was at the root of Silo Studio's exploration of polystyrene, one of the most commonly encountered plastics. Disposable cutlery and tableware are moulded from polystyrene but it is most commonly encountered as peanut-shaped chips or moulded blocks of expanded pellets that are used for packaging. Very light and very strong, but also brittle, polystyrene is regarded as totally ephemeral and disposable. Polystyrene is a thermoplastic and Silo Studio

ABOVE:
NSEPS table
Designed and made by
Silo Studio, UK, 2011

BELOW:
Surface table
Designed by Terence
Woodgate and John Barnard,
Manufactured by Established
& Sons, UK, 2008

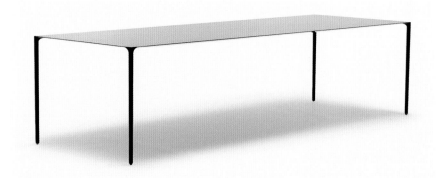

developed its own technique using a steam chamber to cast the pellets in fabric moulds. When heated, the polystyrene pellets swell and adhere to one another, but constricted by the fabric mould they cannot expand in volume. The results are hard, with a dense and heavy mass, quite unlike familiar polystyrene. Silo Studio exploited the newly found durability of polystyrene to fabricate furniture from it, challenging our perceptions of the material and revaluing it.

Like polystyrene, carbon fibre is extremely light, although unlike polystyrene it is not cheap and is extremely strong. Its strength derives from carbon filaments that are suspended in the polymer. Carbon fibre is generally used where high strength-to-weight ratios are necessary, for example in Formula One cars and the aerospace industry. For the same reasons, it is also popular in the design of sports equipment (for example, hockey sticks, fishing rods and bicycle helmets), electronics (such as laptop casings) and technical accessories (for example, photographic tripods). Arguably, it is too highly specified for furniture but this has not perturbed designers including Ron Arad, Marc Newson and Shigeru Ban, who have all used it. Terence Woodgate collaborated with John Barnard, a designer of Formula One cars, to design the Surface table for Established & Sons in 2008. Carbon fibre allowed the tabletop to stretch 3m but to measure only 2mm at its edge.

The Brazilian company Grendene has been making plastic shoes since 1971, and in 1979 it created a brand called Melissa to manufacture design-led footwear and accessories. Melissa shoes are made from a patented non-toxic PVC called Melflex™, designed to be both supple for comfort and durably rigid, and the brand has invited notable designers, usually from outside the world of fashion, to contribute designs including Zaha Hadid, the Campana brothers and Karim Rashid. Their products celebrate plastic as a material and push the boundaries of manufacturing techniques.

BELOW:
Melissa shoes
Designed by Zaha Hadid (left) and Fernando and Humberto Campana (right), Manufactured by Grendene, Brazil, 2008 (left), 2005 (right)

TEXTILES

The defining character of a textile is the presence of spun or twisted threads, originally derived from natural sources but today just as likely to be synthetic. Rather like basketwork, weaving a textile is a process of intermeshing strands of thread, while weaving's cousin, knitting, is a technique of knotting a continuous strand. Both processes give different structural and sensual qualities to the textile and are employed primarily in the clothing and interior design sectors. In our clothes, textiles have the most intimate and lasting relationship with our bodies and are primarily designed for their comfort and thermal qualities. In the home, textiles like carpets, bedding and upholstery also come into contact with our bodies but are principally selected for their decorative as well as their durable characteristics. Further afield we find textiles in vehicle interiors, medical dressings, temporary architecture such as tents and pavilions, and as dynamic mechanical components like the sails of yachts and windsurfers, or parachutes. Textiles, in short, are an adaptable and versatile material that we find everywhere.

Like some of the other materials and techniques that we have already explored, textile is an ancient medium. The earliest surviving woven textiles – Egyptian linens – date from soon after 5000 BC. Cotton fabric appeared in India about 3000 BC and wool some time later in the Near East and Scandinavia, about 1150 BC. Shortly afterwards, about 1000 BC, silk fabrics were developed in China. These represent the principal natural materials used to make textiles to this day, although other natural fibres have been explored, for example hemp and the lustrous gold silk produced by the golden silk orb-weaver spider of Madagascar. Twentieth-century textiles were dominated by new synthetic yarns such as polyester, rayon and nylon, and today designers such as Moritz Waldemeyer are embedding digital technologies into textiles with startling impact.

In this section we will meet some of the designers who are working with textiles in interesting and surprising ways, often by taking them out of their usual contexts or by deliberately "misusing" them to achieve particular effects.

ABOVE:
Spider silk cape (detail)
Made by Simon Peers and
Nicholas Godley, Madagascar,
2011

LEFT:
Costumes for Audi press launch
Designed by Moritz Waldemeyer
and Erevos Aether, UK, 2013

RIPPING YARNS

All woven and knitted textiles are made from yarns or threads, but two young design studios have used yarn to make fascinating and innovative products.

Based in Vienna, mischer'traxler studio is a partnership of Katharina Mischer and Thomas Traxler. They designed their own solar-powered machine that progressively dyes and winds glue-soaked thread around a mould. It starts when the sun rises and stops at sunset, and the speed depends on the sun's strength. The machine makes unique benches with the colour intensity and size of each one dependent on the specific conditions under which it was made. The designers call this project The Idea of a Tree because, like a tree, the objects record their own growth process.

In Sweden, Anton Alvarez uses a remarkable thread-wrapping machine of his own devising to construct furniture and lamps. The machine spins glue-soaked threads in opposing directions from rotating rings. These quickly envelop anything inserted into the rings and bind together individual components such as wood or tubes without the need for conventional joints or screws. The thread layer dries hard, and is both a decorative coating or skin and an intrinsic part of the furniture's structure.

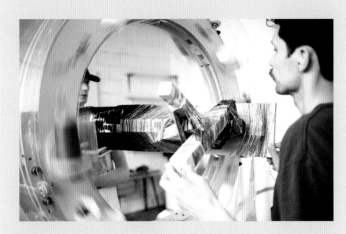

TOP:
The Idea of a Tree
Designed and made by mischer'traxler,
Austria, 2008

ABOVE & RIGHT:
Thread-Wrapping machine and chair
Designed and made by Anton Alvarez,
Sweden, 2012

ABOVE:
Clouds, textile panel system
Designed by Ronan and
Erwan Bouroullec,
Manufactured by Kvadrat,
Denmark, 2009

Textiles have their own tensile strength gained from the fibres from which they are made, but they are not known for their structural rigidity. Rather, they are intended to flow and drape around the human body or as a cover over another form, such as upholstery. The brothers Ronan and Erwan Bouroullec, designers in Paris, have explored textiles' potential as a freestanding structure, working with the Danish manufacturer Kvadrat, which specializes in making woolen wovens and felts. For Kvadrat the brothers designed Clouds, a system of triangulated woolen panels or tiles that can be joined together to make a self-supporting room divider. The system is intended to warm up and humanize rather sterile and bleak modern interiors, such as open-plan offices, and the wool panels also have a beneficial sound insulating quality too.

In Japan, the design studio Nendo worked with a specialist textile manufacturer called the Asahi Kasei Fibers Corporation to develop blown-fabric lanterns. They are made of special long-fibre, non-woven polyester that can be formed by

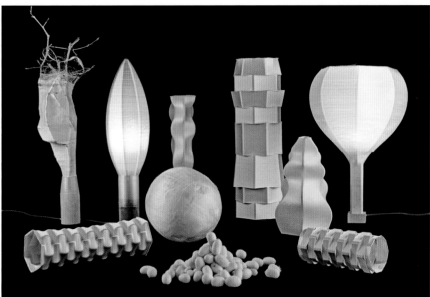

hot pressing. The fabric is light and rip-proof and has its own structural rigidity. The lamps are formed rather like blown glass into seamless one-piece units, and since the process cannot be entirely controlled, each lantern is subtly different. Although synthetic, the lanterns have an organic, natural aesthetic not dissimilar to silk. Royal College of Art student Yasuhiro Suzuki explored the potential of silk to gain structural consistency with visually similar results. During the production of silk textile the cocoons are unwound and the fibre is washed. Suzuki found that if he did not wash the fibres before he spun them around a removable mould, the result was both soft and malleable but also capable of retaining its structure. Silk is strong, heat-retaining and has antibacterial qualities, so perhaps Suzuki's innovation could find interesting and useful applications in medicine, for example moulded dressings. At the Massachusetts Institute of Technology (MIT) designers have worked with silk worms as if they were "biological printers", encouraging them to weave silk over a frame to create a temporary shelter. We are familiar with

ABOVE:
Lanterns
Designed by Nendo,
Manufactured by Asahi
Kasei Fibers Corporation,
Japan, 2009

ABOVE:
Lamps and experimental forms
Designed and made by
Yasuhiro Suzuki, UK, 2014

how we intercede into the natural behaviour of silk worms to get the silk yarn we want to weave into textile, but this is a more collaborative production process with more organic and somewhat random results.

The designer and artist Rowan Mersh has explored the stretch and flexibility of knitted jersey fabric to create non-functional sculptural installations, sometimes on a large, architectural scale but also somewhere between jewellery, clothing and armour to be worn on the body. He works with industrially made textiles and components, exploiting the even and consistent malleability of jersey, for example Helix, a neck piece constructed with approximately 3,000 toothpicks that create twisting DNA-like structures in the fabric.

The designers at BMW also exploited textiles' ability to take on new shapes when they conceived the GINA Light Visionary Model concept car. Unlike the metal (and occasionally plastic) shells of regular cars that are fixed into permanent rigid forms, GINA has a stretched fabric skin over a moveable wire framework. This enables the car to change shape and form depending on conditions, for example to affect the aerodynamics. GINA remains purely a one-off concept that will never be produced but the principle of using hi-tech fabrics to skin vehicles opens up possibilities to reconceive how cars are made. In fact, the idea is not that new: consider the structures of airships such as Zeppelins that ruled the skies a century ago.

ABOVE:
Silk Pavilion
Designed and made by
MIT Media Lab, USA, 2013

TOP RIGHT:
GINA Light Visionary Model concept car
Designed and made by
BMW, Germany, 2008

RIGHT:
Helix
Designed and made by
Rowan Mersh, UK, 2006

7. HUMAN-CENTRED DESIGN & ERGONOMICS

In Chapter 3 we introduced the idea that products need to be "fit for their purpose", and that many products can be thought of as tools because they enhance our abilities by making us stronger or more adept. In this chapter we will explore these ideas further by looking at human-centred design and ergonomics, interchangeable terms that are concerned with the fit between the human user, their equipment and their environment. In other words, human-centred design seeks to optimize our performance, usually by closely studying the ways in which we interact with the world around us. Ergonomics draws on many different disciplines, from sociology to industrial design, and may lead to tiny improvements to everyday items, such as softening the grip on a screwdriver so it is more comfortable to use, or adjustments to large-scale systems, for example the design of traffic flows to improve road safety.

The origins of ergonomics were in the study of workers' activities in factories and how pilots of highly technical new aircraft managed their equipment: by applying a scientific and analytical approach, it was thought people could be made more "machine-like" and therefore more productive, accurate and less at risk of injury through work. As the twentieth century progressed, the idea of the worker as robot has been largely discredited and ergonomics has centred on health, safety and enhancement of individuals, particularly by focusing on allowing for human differences. Ergonomic principles are still very important in the design of working environments such as offices, for example providing optimal sitting positions at desks so workers can avoid muscular-skeletal problems associated with poor posture and painful conditions like carpal tunnel syndrome arising from stresses on the wrists from typing.

A champion of designing around human factors was the American industrial designer Niels Diffrient, who died in 2013. For the company Humanscale, Diffrient designed several innovative office task chairs and in 2007 was described by *Forbes* magazine as the "granddaddy of the ergonomic revolution". How ergonomics has influenced the evolution of task chairs will be explored in more depth in Chapter 10.

As we shall see from the designs that follow, today human-centred design is really about empowerment. Designers are seeking design solutions to problems

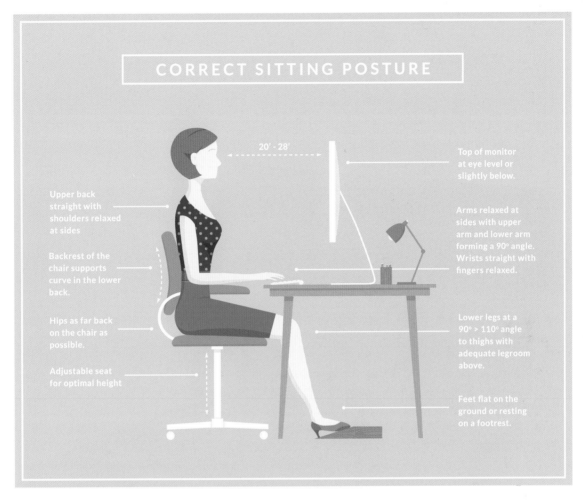

CORRECT SITTING POSTURE

20' - 28'

Top of monitor at eye level or slightly below.

Upper back straight with shoulders relaxed at sides

Arms relaxed at sides with upper arm and lower arm forming a 90° angle. Wrists straight with fingers relaxed.

Backrest of the chair supports curve in the lower back.

Hips as far back on the chair as possible.

Lower legs at a 90° > 110° angle to thighs with adequate legroom above.

Adjustable seat for optimal height

Feet flat on the ground or resting on a footrest.

brought about by old age, incapacity or lack of access to resources through poverty. These are designers who are trying to make tangible improvements to how we experience the world, sometimes for the few but often for the many. For this reason many people describe this approach as "inclusive design", believing that we should all be able to benefit from design, not just the fit, the young or the wealthy. In each case they start with people and their physical interactions with their environments.

We can see ergonomic factors at play in the design of everyday items intended for mass consumption, such as plastic chairs, tableware, kitchen appliances and even electronic equipment like laptop computers. When he designed the N310 notebook for Samsung, Naoto Fukasawa made sure it had smooth edges and a tactile, rubberized casing that invited users' touch. He commented: "People chose things that are the most handy shapes or the shapes that are the most tactually inviting. The same applies to computers and mobile phones. No matter how stylish these objects are if there are sharp corners or surfaces that distract our mind, we become unwilling to interact. In other words while people may enjoy the shape or design of such objects, the body will naturally reject them."

ABOVE:
Correct Sitting Posture diagram.

ABOVE:
N310 mini notebook computer
Designed for Naoto Fukasawa,
Manufactured by Samsung, South Korea, 2009

LEFT:
Tip Ton chair
Designed by Barber Osgerby,
Manufactured by Vitra,
Switzerland, 2011

BELOW:
Waver chair
Designed by Konstantin Grcic,
Manufactured by Vitra,
Switzerland, 2011

Fukasawa began his design by considering how the laptop would be touched and held. Similarly, two chairs designed by Barber Osgerby incorporated observations about how people sit in different situations. The Tip Ton chair has a rocker-style base that tips up at the front, allowing sitters to tilt the chair slightly forward for conversation or to eat at a table. The chair they designed for the Bodleian Library in Oxford has a broader seat than most chairs, giving comfortable "squirm room" to library researchers who may be seated for long periods of time. The Waver chair was designed by Konstantin Grcic in 2011 and borrows from the visual language of sports equipment; the webbed fabric, for example. The slung fabric seat is precisely cut to fit the human body for the best ergonomic support, which is further enhanced with neck, lumbar and seat cushions. Ergonomic thinking is embedded in the chair's design, yet it does not look like a piece of specialist ergonomic furniture in the way earlier designs did, such as kneeling stools that sought to improve posture. It is clear that an interest in ergonomics need not lead a furniture designer to design something akin to medical equipment. Even where there are medical considerations in the design of an item, for example a wheelchair, the design can emphasize action and the chair can empower the user, rather than stigmatize them by drawing negative attention to their differences.

WHEELCHAIRS

A look at five wheelchairs shows the similarities and, crucially, the differences that arise when designers approach the same problem from a variety of perspectives. They each aimed to enable mobility for a chair-bound person but their different priorities shaped the outcomes in specific ways.

Mex-x and Chair 4 Life wheelchairs

The Mex-x is a folding chair designed for children that comes with a selection of changeable wheel guards enabling a child to have a sense of ownership and individuality. It still looks like a conventional wheelchair with large side wheels. The Chair 4 Life looks quite different, and was designed with the intention of "seeing the child, not the chair". It was designed for children aged 4 to 18 and to be adaptable to their use over time. A key feature is its vertical lift, allowing users to have eye-to-eye contact with their peers: a profound understanding by the designers of the psychological as well as physical contribution possible through inclusive design thinking.

Balance and Worldmade sport wheelchairs

Whereas the Mex-x is designed for everyday and general use, the Balance sport wheelchair is for a very specific context: sports activities where players need both hands free, for example basketball. The chair can be steered by simply tilting the body left or right and the brakes are applied by leaning backwards, leaving the hands free to play the game. The inward slanting wheels give the users stability and maneuverability and the exposed, lightweight frame draws on the visual appearance of highly engineered sports bikes. High-performance wheelchairs like this can be expensive, but there are also lower cost models that share the same basic form. David Constantine, a noted industrial designer and user of a wheelchair himself, designed the Worldmade sport wheelchair to be as low-cost as possible (about one tenth of the cost of other models), in a bid to give access to sport to most wheelchair users, even in low-income countries. It shows how ergonomic and economic considerations can come together in inclusive design.

Carbon Black wheelchair

Andrew Slorance is also a wheelchair user and the Carbon Black chair he designed is quite different again. He chose to make it of carbon fibre: very light, extremely strong and possible to mould into ergonomic forms, which together mean the chair can be discreet and not dominate its user's appearance. He incorporated features such as quick-release mechanisms so it can be easily and efficiently folded and stowed, and integral LED lights to guide the user in the dark. Slorance was determined to make the chair as different as possible from the utilitarian and medical chairs he grew up with, and he succeeded.

LEFT:
Balance sport wheelchair
Designed by Eric Larson, Ricky Biddle, Ben Shao and Austin Cliffe, USA, 2013

ABOVE LEFT:
Chair 4 Life wheelchair
Designed by Renfrew Group for the NHS National Innovation Centre, UK, 2013

ABOVE:
Carbon Black wheelchair
Designed by Andrew Slorance, Manufactured by I Imagine, UK, 2011

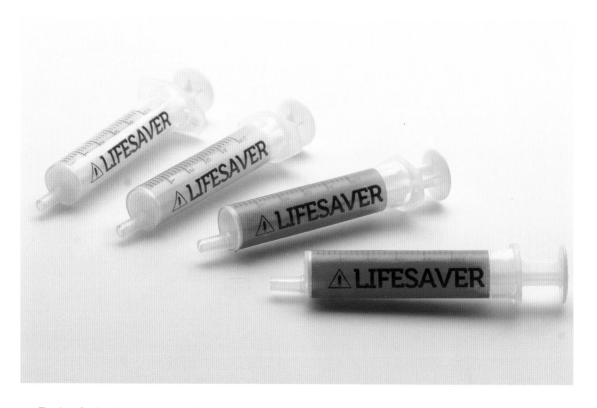

Design for healthcare is one of the most rewarding sectors for inclusive designers, because advances in medicine and technology enable innovative design thinking to take place. There are also many seemingly intractable problems for designers to address. One such is the reuse of syringes. Of the 17 billion injections given each year, an estimated seven billion are delivered with reused syringes causing widespread but avoidable infection and deaths. The ABC (A Behaviour Changing) syringe was conceived by David Swann, exploiting carbon-dioxide sensitive ink. Once the injection has been administered, the interior of the barrel is exposed to air, which activates the ink and causes the syringe to turn dark red in just 60 seconds, clearly indicating it should not be re-used and, in any case, making it difficult to do so. Red was chosen as it is universally associated with risk, and the addition of the ink to a standard syringe form is both easy and economical, meaning the syringe may be able to make a real impact in countries where medical resources are limited.

Closer to home, the National Health Service together with the Design Council initiated the Design Bugs Out initiative as a challenge to designers to address the problem of infections, such as MRSA, picked up by patients in hospitals. PearsonLloyd redesigned the commode, a mobile toilet for those patients unable to get to bathroom facilities. By separating the seat shell from the frame, the commode can be more easily maintained and repaired and the number of components is reduced. Importantly the design minimizes joints, crevices and contact points

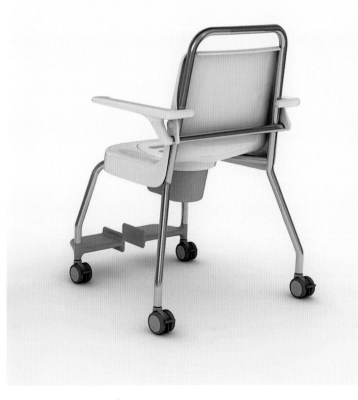

between the shell and frame, making it easy and quick to clean and avoiding places where germs can build up. It may be an unglamorous design challenge, but it is one where thinking about the needs of the users – both the patients and the clinicians – is paramount to delivering a successful and worthwhile product.

Sometimes lateral thinking by designers can open up a world of possibilities, which is the case with an anti-diarrhoea kit designed by PI Global for Cola Life, an independent not-for-profit aid organization working with Coca-Cola. The kits, which include simple medical items such as hydration salts and measuring jugs, are designed in wedge-shaped packs that fit between crated Coca-Cola bottles, allowing the medical charity to piggy-back on the well-established distribution channels of the global giant and so reach those who need the kits most.

In a sense, the Coca-Cola crates and their system of distribution are a kind of organizational framework or skeleton that enables the existence of the anti-diarrhoea kits. An exoskeleton is an external support frame or shell familiar in insect life, unlike the internal bone structures of mammals like us. The analogy of an exoskeleton is a useful way to consider how rethinking organizational delivery, or physical structures, can help solve a design issue. For example, there are medical conditions where devices similar to exoskeletons are beneficial, to give strength and support to weak or damaged limbs. The WREX (Wilmington Robotic Exoskeleton) 3D-printed arms combine ergonomic understanding of the human body with computer-aided design and manufacture: a marriage of organic and digital design principles. They are very suitable for a child's use, as they are much lighter than metal equivalents; and since the components are 3D printed, they can be updated easily as the child grows.

BELOW:
WREX (Wilmington Robotic Exoskeleton) 3D-printed arms
Designed and manufactured by Tariq Rahman and Whitney Sample of Nemours/Alfred 1 duPont Hospital with Stratasys Ltd, USA, 2012

CHILD VISION GLASSES

It is not known where spectacles were invented, or by whom. Marco Polo is said to have seen them on his travels to China in 1270, and the earliest examples were seen in Europe at about the same time. The basic principle of glass (and latterly, plastic) optical lenses held in front of the eyes to correct vision has remained the same even if their design and manufacture have been refined. Therefore, we can think of spectacles as a very early user-centred design innovation that still has common currency. The Child Vision glasses were designed to give access to spectacles to the estimated 60 million short-sighted children in the developing world. Cheap and easy to manufacture, each pair is fitted with silicone oil-filled lenses, the thickness of which can be adjusted by squeezing an applicator fitted to the arm of the glasses to add or release fluid. The innovation is that identical spectacles can be mass-produced, bringing down their cost, but customized to suit the specific sight of each user. With implications for a child's ability to read and benefit from education, the Child Vision glasses truly are an example of design's ability to empower people.

ABOVE:
Child Vision glasses
Designed by the Centre for Vision in the
Developing World and Goodwin Hartshorn,
UK, 2012

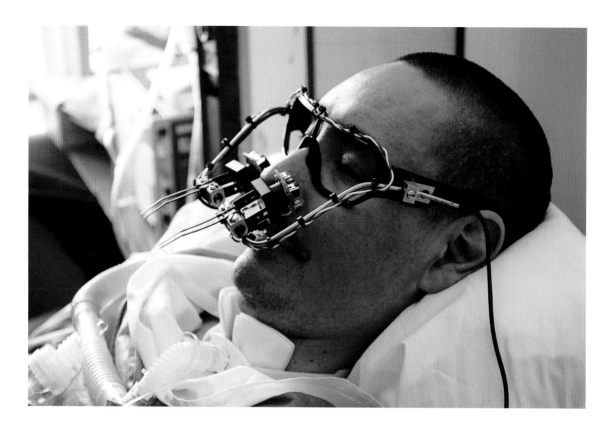

Sometimes a person can be so severely paralyzed that they are only able to move their eyes. This is what happened to Tony Quan, a Los Angeles publisher, activist and graffiti artist, who contracted ALS (a form of motor neurone disease) that left him almost completely paralyzed in 2003. Together with software developers, open-source computer coders and specialist technical experts, Quan was able to design the EyeWriter. The device combines a pair of low-cost eye-tracking glasses with software that enables Quan to draw using his eyes. The EyeWriter is comparable with speech simulators as it uses digital technology to enable a patient to communicate. What is most remarkable about the EyeWriter is that it is an open-source collaboration between designers, engineers and computer experts, each bringing their own expertise to create a life-affirming product with implications for numerous sufferers of paralysis.

The EyeWriter is an extreme response to an extreme condition and fortunately most of us do not require such elaborate or personalized design solutions to our problems. Yet aging populations mean that poor sight and even total blindness are increasingly commonplace. Many familiar appliances are adapted to help, and frequently a simple design change can make all the difference. For example, clocks and playing cards are made with large numbers, and telephones have enlarged

ABOVE:
EyeWriter
Developed by members of Free Art and Technology, openFrameworks, Graffiti Research Lab, The Ebeling Group and Tony Quan, USA, 2009

buttons, to aid clarity. But sometimes users resist these products, as they can feel stigmatized by them. Simon Kinneir interviewed many people with impaired vision to discover how they used their kitchens and what their priorities were for kitchenware designed with them in mind. With this information he designed a range of kitchenware including tumblers, mugs, chopping boards, plates, cutlery and saucepans that he called Subtle Sensory Feedback. His intention was to be as inclusive as possible, designing items that would have mass appeal and not look like niche products for the disabled. Yet each item was designed with subtle additions that could help them be used by the visually impaired. These were mostly tactile, such as a thinner area of ceramic on the side of a mug that would become hot faster than the rest, so a user could feel when the mug was correctly filled. Kinneir used visual clues such as strong graphic patterns in black and white as decoration on a chopping board that also guide a user towards channels intended to help position a knife. Even aural cues were useful: Kinneir added a tiny distortion to a saucepan lid so it rattled when the contents was boiling, helping a partially sighted cook to know how a meal was progressing. Kinneir's project shows that the best user-centred design is underplayed, sensitive, based on observation of behaviour to identify needs, and inclusive.

ABOVE:
Subtle Sensory Feedback kitchenware
Designed by Simon Kinneir, UK, 2013

8. DIGITAL DESIGN

It is sometimes said that we are living through a digital revolution, an "information age" shaped by computing power and the advent of the "virtual world". In this chapter we will explore how digital technologies impact on the design process and the opportunities they present to designers.

Their impact is twofold. On the one hand, digital technologies have transformed the design process itself; they have changed how designers go about creating their designs. On the other hand, computers have affected a sea change in how products are physically made once they have been designed. Arguably the digital realm has a third impact, transforming the ways in which we, the consumers, experience design. Since we are discussing a number of fast-moving, cutting-edge technologies, much of what is produced remains speculative rather than widespread and we will return to the potential impact they may have on the future in a subsequent chapter.

How has the digital world changed the design process? In the not-so-distant past design studios of all disciplines would have been dominated by drawing boards and model-making workshops: design was an analogue, mechanical, hand-driven exercise. Today, many design studios are filled with ranks of computer workstations and look like call centres or bank trading rooms. This is because many (though, crucially, not all) design processes happen virtually, on screen. Fewer designers start with an initial hand-drawn sketch or cardboard maquette because software has been developed to create two- and three-dimensional models that can be adapted, tested, scaled up or down, and even rendered photo-realistically, all in the virtual world without ever existing physically. Possibly the only design discipline to buck this trend is fashion, where working with real textiles at the scale of the human body persists.

The design process is speeded up with digital modelling because designs can be shared and tested quickly and easily. In earlier chapters we explored the development of both Konstantin Grcic's MYTO chair (see Chapter 1) and the Olympic relay torch designed by Barber Osgerby (see Chapter 2) . Even though the first design ideas were developed through models, very quickly the design was digitized and ultimately these files became the blueprint for the production process.

Most software works on the principle of parametricism, whereby designers are able to identify co-ordinate points or nodes on their design and prescribe certain relational constraints between them to ensure that, as changes are made to one part of the design, the rest of the model is adjusted accordingly. Parametricism is an algorithmic, mathematical expression of design drawing and is best used as a tool to interpret and process the result of hand-drawn sketches, rather than as a

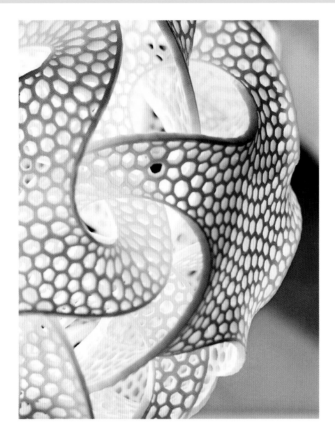

generator of original design ideas. Prototypes, sketch models and even people can be digitized using 3D scanners to ensure that the digital model is based on physical reality. After all, a purely digital drawing or rendering can appear soulless and simulated because it is distanced from the hand and eye.

Digital technologies have completely transformed how designs are prototyped. In the past, models were made by hand, but in 1984 the first 3D printer appeared. Working in tandem with the design software, these printers allowed designers and architects to quickly and accurately produce three-dimensional scale or 1:1 models of their designs, giving physical existence to their virtual presence. The printers work on the principle that the 3D design is divided into very thin horizontal layers that are gradually laid down, one on top of the previous layer. Gradually the object is built up in an additive process. Very quickly designers and manufacturers of 3D printers realized the technology had potential beyond the prototyping stage and could be used to fabricate complete products. One of the first designers to experiment with making products with 3D printers was Ron Arad in the 1990s.

ABOVE LEFT:
Quin light fitting
Designed by
Bathsheba Grossman,
Manufactured by
Materialise.MGX,
Belgium, 2005

ABOVE RIGHT:
Printing with a 3D printer
Bangalore, India, 2013

3D-DESIGN SOFTWARE

The most frequently used design software packages all first appeared in the mid-1990s.

- Rhino was developed by Robert McNeel and Associates in 1994. Rhino uses a non-rational basis spline (NURBS) mathematical model to generate curves and surfaces useful for industrial design, architecture, vehicle design, jewellery and graphics. Third-party developers have introduced tools that plug into Rhino, such as Grasshopper, a parametric modelling tool popular with architects.
- Solidworks was developed by Jon Hirschtick in 1995 and is now produced by Dassault Systèmes SolidWorks Corp. Solidworks uses parametrics to generate solid models, emphasizing their mass and parts. The original aim of its developers was to design easy-to-use and affordable software for Windows operating systems and Solidworks has become particularly popular in the education sector for these reasons.
- Maya was developed by Alias Systems Corporation in 1998 and has been produced by Autodesk Inc. since 2005. Unlike Solidworks and Rhino, Maya did not originate as a tool for industrial designers and architects but as an animation tool for the movie and video game industries. It is used to create interactive 3D applications for games, and special programmes have been developed to simulate fur, hair, cloth, smoke and explosions, which can be useful effects for both animators and designers.

PRINCIPLE 3D PRINTING TECHNOLOGIES

All 3D printers use digitized designs in the form of computer files to control their processes. The machines use one of two techniques: one method involves building up very thin layers of material on a bed, the other intersects laser beams, fired into a tank, to fuse a liquid into a solid.

- FDM (fused deposition modelling) is an extrusion process that lays down layers of thermoplastics, eutectic (easily melted) metals, modelling clay, silicone and porcelain.
- EBF3 (electron beam freeform fabrication) was developed by NASA and uses electron beams to melt a molten pool on a metal substrate in a vacuum. It is able to build complex self-supporting wire-frame structures without moulds or dies.
- DMLS (direct metal laser sintering) sinters metal at points in space defined by a virtual 3D model. Sintering is a process of forming a solid mass of material by heat or pressure, but not melting it. The atoms diffuse between particles of the material and fuse them together.
- EBM (electron-beam melting) and SLM (selective laser melting) can both be used to form metals, including titanium, stainless steel and aluminium.
- SHS (selective heat sintering) and SLS (selective laser sintering) are techniques of fusing granular thermoplastic powders, while SLS can also fuse metal and ceramic powders.
- PP (plaster-based 3D printing) is a technique that uses an inkjet printer head to move over a bed of plaster powder introducing a binding agent in layers to create the three-dimensional form. Other related powder-bed techniques are SLS and SLM (described above).
- LOM (laminated object manufacture) fuses layers of paper, metal foil and plastic film to create objects.

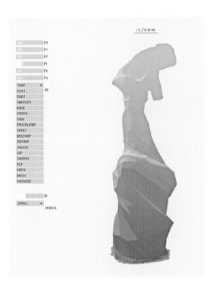

Arad's early experiments extracted frozen frames from a digital animation of a bouncing spring form, to create an endless variety of related vase and lamp forms based on tense spirals. He had immediately identified the correlation between the dynamic digital design and its ability to generate unique finished artifacts. The Belgian firm Materialise is one of the principal makers of 3D printing technology and its .MGX division creates a collection of lighting and furniture by a roster of designers including Assa Ashuach, Amanda Levete and Patrick Jouin celebrating the unique fabrication that is only possible with additive manufacturing. Unlike casts or moulds, which do not permit undercuts or forms within forms, 3D-printed artifacts can be extremely complex and appear almost irrational, yet they can be manufactured as single units that do not require assembly. Much of the .MGX collection is based on parametric algorithms and celebrate their computer-generated aesthetic.

More recently, in 2012, London-based designer Matthew Plummer-Fernandez experimented with scanning everyday vessels like cleaning-fluid bottles and watering cans, and using the scans to generate new abstracted, parametric forms that he fabricated with 3D printers. The new vessels are not intended to be functional or contain anything more than the digital data that generated them.

Early 3D printers were constrained by the size of the beds in which to make objects and by the brittle resins they used. Since then, many variations have been developed at all scales.

In China and the Netherlands, for example, massive printers have been built that can print entire houses in a matter of hours. The Chinese printers measured 10m x 6.6m and sprayed layers of concrete and construction waste to build houses for just £3,000. The components were made off-site before being assembled. In Amsterdam, DUS Architects are printing plastic bricks on-site that are then connected like units of Lego to build a house.

If we can print entire buildings, what else is possible? A well-established manufacturer of the technology, 3D Systems, has launched ChefJet printers

capable of printing sugar confectionery and is working on starch-based printers that will be capable (theoretically, at least) of printing hamburgers. The Chefjet is not fast – it can print layers of sugar one-inch thick each hour – but the results are precise and endlessly variable. Like food colouring, the composition of inks used in regular printers are regulated so they are safe for people to use. Harvard Business School student Grace Choi exploited this to disrupt the cosmetics industry by hacking existing scanning and 3D printing technologies to print her own make-up. Her mini home-printer, called Mink, takes colour codes from colours she finds in photographs on the Internet and uses them to mix and print precise colour powders to use as make-up. The device makes it possible to match cosmetics to exact shades of clothing in an instant.

So we can print engineered, rigid structures, food and make-up: what else is possible? Why not 3D-print soft materials? That was the challenge Scott E. Hudson at the Human-Computer Interaction Institute, part of Carnegie Mellon University

TOP:
3D-printed house
Designed and built by
WinSun, China, 2014

ABOVE:
3D-printed confectionery
Designed and manufactured
by 3D Systems, USA, 2014

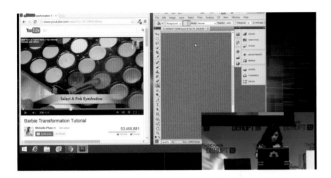

and Disney Research in Pittsburgh, set himself. He designed a device that can print with wool yarn by felting it to the layers below, to create soft forms from 3D digital designs. His demonstration example was a small teddy bear, but he also showed how the machine could cocoon felt around hardware or substrates to add other interactions to the products, such as motion or sound.

A great advantage of digital design and manufacture is that it can take place on a micro scale. The texture of sharkskin, which has tiny sharp "teeth" known as denticles, has been well studied. The denticles create minute fluctuations in the water currents around the shark that aid its swimming, and designers have tried to mimic this for the texture of swimsuits. Now, scientists at Harvard University have succeeded in scanning sharkskin and reproducing the denticles using 3D printing. Each denticle is just 0.15mm long, which is too small for even the most refined printer, so the simulation has denticles 10 times that size. Nevertheless, they show measurable improvements to water flow in tests.

Artificial snakeskin is an example of biomimicry, which is the adaptation of naturally occurring forms or materials by designers. Digital design and manufacture also enables individual customization of products and this has major implications for medicine. This is particularly so for the production of casts to set broken bones, because each person and every injury has unique characteristics. Conventional plaster casts are cumbersome and restrict airflow to the skin, so New Zealand designer Jake Evill designed a 3D-printed cast system inspired by the cellular structure of bone. The casts are like exoskeletons, generated from x-rays and scans of the injured limb, and are perforated by holes to aid airflow and reduce weight. The holes are smaller and the cast is strongest around the injury

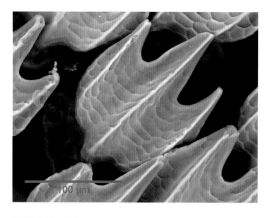

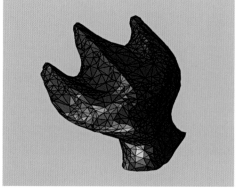

ABOVE & LEFT:
Scan of sharkskin, 3D model and 3D-printed denticles
Designed by Professor George Lauder,
Harvard University, USA, 2014

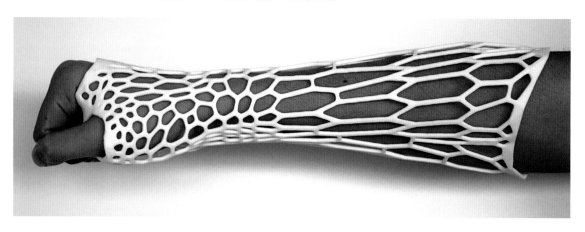

ABOVE:
Cortex 3D-printed medical cast
Designed by Jake Evill, New Zealand, 2013

ABOVE & RIGHT:
**3Doodler, 3D-printing pen
and model outcome**
Designed by Peter Dilworth
and Maxwell Bogue,
Manufactured by Wobbleworks,
USA, 2013

area, to support and protect it, and bespoke casts can be printed for each patient. Designers are exploring other ways in which 3D printing can be applied to medical conditions, including orthodontic and orthopaedic implants, artificial blood vessels and even specialist surgical equipment.

Digital design software enables designers to accurately model their ideas in the virtual realm and communicate and share these designs with manufacturers. Additive manufacturing hardware that has grown out of rapid prototyping presents a radical alternative to conventional casting, moulding or carving technologies and soon will have an impact on mass production. At present, experimental design tends towards the digital customization of products to be made in situ or for specific individuals. The next generation of printers will be smaller and more adaptable, like the 3Doodler which claims to be the world's first 3D-printing pen. It does not require a computer or a separate printer, as the pen extrudes plastic when it is moved through space to create instant, freehand, three-dimensional sketches. In Chapter 12 we will see how the digital revolution enables everyone to design and make their own work, through hacking and home-printing.

9. THE IMPACT OF DESIGN

At the beginning of this book I defined design as a process of solving problems, and as an agent of positive change, since all designers are seeking improvements to the world as it stands today. In this chapter we will look more closely at the impact that design can make on the world; the good things that design can effect but also the bad.

Everything that is designed, made, consumed and ultimately disposed of is part of a huge matrix of cause and effect. This matrix is complex because there are few clearly "right" or "wrong" products since they are all open to different interpretations depending on your point of view. A product may have an obvious beneficial impact on society but its fabrication or disposal could also be a polluter. Until now we have focused on designers' roles in shaping design, but in this chapter arguably it is us, the consumers of goods, who are equally implicated in design's impact because without our demand there would be less need for more products.

The insatiable demand for more goods, and the techniques of industrial production that feed markets with cheap mass-manufactured products, has made humankind both greedy and careless. We are used to expecting to get what we want, when we want it, and our political and economic systems have pandered to us by encouraging consumption of every type of product. Entire sectors, such as cosmetics, have arisen to fulfill man-made, spurious needs that did not exist before. As we saw with the automobile industry in the mid-twentieth century, planned obsolescence (see Chapter 4)– the deliberate styling of products to go out of fashion, or for components to fail quickly – generated constant desire for replacements when in fact they were seldom necessary. Dazzled by our capacity to consume, we remain stubbornly blind to the consequences, despite the evidence surrounding us. If we were able to double the life of products, at a stroke we would halve their environmental impact. This is a fairly unambitious target yet our greed for novel products makes it unlikely to be met.

One of the most blatant and shocking indictments of our greed is the huge areas of ocean where scientists have recorded increasing concentrations of plastic waste, trapped by currents and prevailing winds. These so-called "garbage patches" are thought by some to be as big as entire continents and exist in all the large seas of the world. They are difficult to measure and even to detect since they are largely made up of minute plastic fragments known as nurdles floating below the surface and concentrations of chemicals given off as plastics degrade. Larger items, such as discarded fishing nets, also get caught in the currents. This pollution, which impacts upon marine life and through them enters our food chain, is the result of our addiction to plastic products and packaging, and our willful and negligent disposal of them.

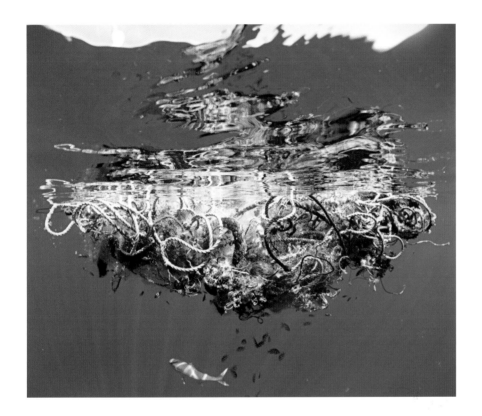

Clearly the designers of many of the products that end up in these polluted seas intended them for higher purposes. Toothbrushes, for example, have a positive impact by improving the dental health of millions of users, but they are designed with short lifespans and without consideration of recyclability. They often combine several different plastics that are inseparable, and the entire product must be replaced when only one area, the bristles, becomes worn out. Designers, with manufacturers, have a duty to challenge this profligate waste, but there are few commercial incentives to do so.

How can designers encourage us to be more responsible, and how can they improve the design of products to reduce their negative impacts? One way is for them to reduce their environmental footprint by decreasing the quantity of materials needed to make products. Another is by seeking out natural or biodegradable materials in place of synthetics or oil-based plastics, and in a previous chapter we explored how designers are sometimes also material researchers. Designers can also encourage imaginative recycling, such as the Sea Chair and the Bottle Light.

SEA CHAIR

The Sea Chair was designed and made by Studio Swine and Kieren Jones in 2011. It is a simple three-legged stool entirely made of recycled plastic nurdles dredged from the sea off Cornwall or recovered from its beaches. The stool can only make a tiny, inconsequential, impact on the quantity of plastic pollution in the oceans, but it can serve as an example of how the challenge could be met through design. Its young designers worked out how to collect and process the plastic at sea, lessons that could be easily scaled up to industrial levels if there was a will to do so. They even published open-source designs for their system so others could replicate it. In this instance, designers are addressing a negative impact of design with a symbolic gesture, but one that is grounded in hard facts and with potential to make a positive impact.

ABOVE:
Sea chair
Designed and made by Studio
Swine and Kieren Jones,
UK, 2011

BOTTLE LIGHT

A remarkable instance of the reuse of plastic bottles is from Brazil and was an innovation by a mechanic rather than a trained designer. Alfredo Moser observed how light refracts through water-filled bottles so he cut holes through his roof tiles and installed them, with half the bottle hanging in the room below and half open to the sky. A little added bleach keeps the water clear and a polyester resin seal stops the rain from leaking around the bottles. The Bottle Lights illuminate dark interiors for free, where electricity supply may not be reliable or even available. Depending on the strength of the sun, each bottle can emit light comparable to that of 40- to 60-watt electric light bulbs. Reusing the plastic bottles like this is an imaginative exploitation of an unintentional characteristic they possess – their capacity to refract light. The plastic gains value and permanence rather than becoming wastefully disposable and an agent of pollution. This is significant enough but there are other more profound impacts. Light sources like this bring definite improvements to living standards because they allow people to live and work more easily and, crucially, they aid study because it is possible to see to read and write. So it is not unreasonable to suggest that the simple Bottle Light gives deprived people better access to life-changing education. Moser's idea has caught on across the planet, with schemes to install them as far afield as Fiji, the Philippines, Argentina and Tanzania. Moser shows us we can all apply design thinking for our mutual benefit.

ABOVE:
Bottle light
Designed by Alfredo Moser,
Brazil, 2002

The success of the Bottle Light demonstrates how low-tech solutions can make a real difference. The artist Olafur Eliasson, known for his light installations, has designed a simple solar-powered LED lamp for developing nations where electrical supply is absent or erratic. Design makes a positive impact when designers tackle basic human needs like this. The delivery of essential services such as clean water is certainly aided by design thinking, for example the innovative and extremely low-cost Kyoto Box, designed by the Kenyan-based Norwegian designer Jon Bøhmer. The device is simply a silver-foil-covered box that reflects sunlight onto a second box, painted black to absorb heat. Very quickly it can reach 80°C, a sufficient temperature to sterilize drinking water and cook food. It is named after the Kyoto international environmental agreement, as it is a sustainable alternative to wood-fired cooking (with the concomitant deforestation and CO_2 emissions) in remote regions of the developing world.

Some human rights are more complex, such as the right to be educated, but design can make very positive contributions here too. The One Laptop Per Child project is an ambitious attempt to bring high-tech computing within reach of even the poorest or most isolated children in the world. Its aim is to supply each child with a rugged, low-cost XO laptop computer, complete with bespoke software and connectivity to promote self-empowered learning. Costs are kept low by simplifying parts of the machine such as the screen and selling large quantities to education ministries for distribution to school-age children. To date, 2.4 million children and their teachers have XO computers worldwide.

LEFT:
Kyoto Box solar-powered cooker
Designed by Jon Bøhmer
Manufactured by Kyoto Energy, Kenya, 2009

Without a doubt one of the most negative impacts design can have is through the design of warfare. But the right to defend oneself means even the design of weaponry is morally ambivalent. It is easier to approve of innovations by designers to counter the effects of warfare. Landmines are especially insidious weapons because they are self-operating and can lie active but hidden for many decades after they have been laid. Most victims of landmines are civilians and since 1997 their use has been banned in much of the world. Yet unquantified numbers of mines remain at large, generally in less-developed parts of the globe that were former conflict zones. Because most mines are hidden and forgotten, clearing minefields is dangerous, time-consuming and expensive.

This is the context for Massoud Hassani's remarkable Mine Kafon, a low-cost mine-clearing device. Hassani originates from Afghanistan where a staggering 30 million landmines are estimated to cover a quarter of the country. The device is simply a central core holding 220 bamboo legs with circular plastic feet. Like a giant tumbleweed, the wind blows it across the land and its weight detonates the mines it touches. Hassani estimates each device can detonate 10 mines at a cost of a few pounds each, compared with £780 for the conventional disposal of each mine. The Mine Kafon is a brilliant application of bio-mimicry to solve the most brutal predicament we have created for ourselves. By simple means it enables people to reclaim their land, their safety, their livelihoods and their future: what better impact can designers hope to make?

ABOVE:
Mine Kafon landmine-clearing device
Designed by Massoud Hassani,
The Netherlands, 2011

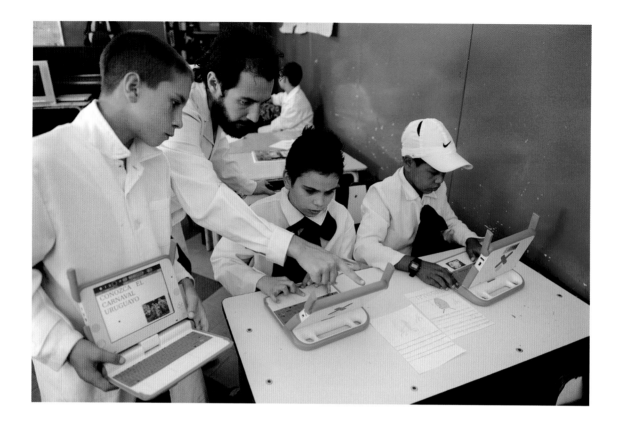

It is not only plastic products that can become pollutants. As electronic gadgets proliferate, electrical waste is fast becoming a major problem, particularly in those developing countries to which the First World exports its defunct appliances. In Ghana, for example, informal recycling of electrical components can pose serious health risks. Electrical wires are burned to recover the valuable copper inside. The wires are necessary to operate the devices, and must be encased in something for safety, but designers and manufacturers of these appliances give inadequate thought to how they will be processed at the end of their operational lives. The Esource, designed by Hal Watts, is a low-tech electrical-wire recycling scheme that is safer than burning the cables. It relies on easily accessed technology, a bicycle and water to separate the copper from its coating, and since unburned copper is more valuable, it gives the recyclers an enhanced income as well as greater safety. Esource is a small-scale, local intervention that could have a significant impact.

ABOVE:
XO laptop computer
Designed by Yves Béhar
of Fuseproject for OLPC &
Quanta Computer Inc.,USA,
2005

So far we have seen design responses to problems largely caused by mass production and over-consumption in the industrialized world. These problems are out of sight for most of us, as we tend to export them to developing nations. Design can offer solutions to these human-made problems but it can also tackle environmental issues that many people face, regardless of their wealth. Earthquakes, for example, occur in many parts of the globe, and as population densities increase they can wreak havoc for many people. An estimated 300 million children face danger because their schools are built on rift lines but are unable to withstand serious tremors. A team of Israeli designers developed a portable earthquake-proof school desk, strong enough to be a shelter from falling masonry but light enough to be manoeuvered by children. As an example of design conceived not to make profit but to improve lives, the table is exemplary. It sits beside innovative design responses to natural disasters such as the architect Shigeru Ban's emergency shelters built with cardboard tubes.

BELOW:
Earthquake proof table
Designed by Arthur Brutter
and Ido Bruno,
Manufactured by AD Merez
Industries Ltd, Israel, 2011

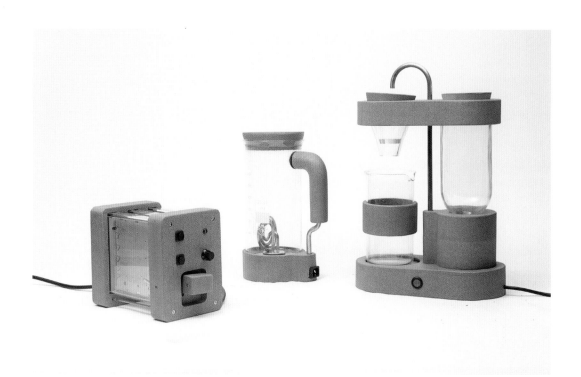

Numerous designs seek to make positive impacts on problems, usually man-made and ironically often the by-product of the success of other designs. Recycling materials and upcycling components can take place on a local scale (explored in more depth in Chapter 12) but re-conceiving the entire design, manufacture and distribution of mobile telephones around ethical principles requires an entirely bigger scale of response; this, however, was the ambitious intention of the Fairphone. Tobacco products are perhaps not strictly speaking designed products, but they owe much of their global success to the seductive imagery of their advertising, branding and packaging that undoubtedly are designed. Increasingly, legislation is appearing that strips away the power of tobacco branding, insisting instead on a type of anti-design, generic appearance for cigarette packets. Leading the field is Australia where all cigarettes are now sold in the same green-brown packages bearing graphic images of tobacco-related illnesses and health warnings. Sometimes the most potent positive impact of design is to remove signs of design altogether.

OPPOSITE TOP:
Upcycled kitchen appliances
Designed by Re-Do Studio,
UK, 2011

OPPOSITE BOTTOM:
Fairphone mobile telephone
Designed by Bas van Abel
Manufactured by Fairphone,
The Netherlands, 2013

ABOVE:
Australian tobacco packaging
2012

10. DESIGN EVOLUTION CASE STUDIES

Most of this book has been concerned with the stages of the design process undertaken by designers and manufacturers, and it can sometimes seem as if each design takes place independently of all others, especially so those that are innovative and shift paradigms and our expectations. But in reality most designs are part of continua and very many are defined, at least in part, by the context of their sector, by the expectations of their market, and by the way in which they are most likely to be used.

In this chapter we will examine how five varied design types have evolved over time, which will give us insight into the influence of context for designers and help us see design as an evolutionary process rather than one of miraculous inception. Corporate identities, logos and brands are our most immediate and insistent experiences of many products, often shaped by graphic designers. The London bus, however, is the result of a century of public transport design influencing the patterns of metropolitan life. Modern office work, and equipment such as computers that goes with it, have demanded the evolution of specialist task chairs. Computing has also affected our leisure time in many ways, not least the development of computer games and the consoles that control them. And specialized sportswear has crossed over into the mainstream fashion market in the form of the training shoe.

CORPORATE IDENTITY

Corporate identities, trademarks and logos largely arose during the later part of the nineteenth century as mass-produced goods proliferated. As their manufacturers sought to differentiate their goods from those of rivals and secure their investments, they turned to legal protection such as patents and registered trademarks. Brand identities, most often in the form of logos and trade names, became the foot soldiers fighting to popularize products and maintain their ascendency in crowded markets. Many of the earliest brands persist to this day, often in the food and drink industries, such as Coca-Cola (patented in 1887) and Heinz (manufacturing food products since 1869).

Brands are, in effect, promises of quality made to consumers by manufacturers so corporate identities can be complex and multilayered but must also be instantly comprehended. Take, for example, Levi Strauss & Co., founded in San Francisco in 1853. Today it is a fashion brand but it is infused with the memory of the original workwear made by the company, such as reinforcing rivets to strengthen seams in the clothes, hard-wearing cotton denim and imagery of pioneers such as cowboys and gold-miners in the labelling and advertising. In this instance the brand is much more than the company's name or a graphic device. In fact, Levi's strives hard to associate itself with key American values: freedom and success through hard work. The brand's subliminal message is "these aren't just jeans, they are a way of life".

Corporate identities are the most blatant expression of capitalist values and it is therefore not surprising that many of the most ubiquitous, long-lasting and successful brands come from the USA. Brand values may be determined in the boardroom but designers give them shape and form. The designer's task is to ensure the brand's values are represented consistently in every way we experience them. For fashion houses, it is not just the clothes themselves that must be appropriate for the brand, but the labelling inside them must carry the same values, together with the character of the store we visit, the carrier-bag we take away with our purchase, the advertising that enticed us in the first place, and even the virtual presence of the brand online. Designers define house styles that control the precise ways in which logos can be used in all circumstances, determining their exact positioning, colour, size and relation to other visual elements such as text copy within an advertisement. In the design of products and retail environments adherence to the house style will also entail choices of materials and finishes. Corporate identities are also frequently used away from the products they represent, such as for a sponsorship deal. Formula One racing teams are heavily sponsored and here the appearance of the sponsor's brand must contend with the speed and action of the sport, as well as complementing racing's own "brand values". An energy drink like Red Bull has similar values of strength, endurance and activity to Formula One, and the design of their car's Red Bull livery strives to enforce this.

A challenge for many publishers is the seismic shift away from tangible printed editions to the ephemeral digital realm. This is most acute for news media that, by necessity, must be at the forefront of opinion and use of technology to maintain

BELOW LEFT:
Levi Strauss & Co branding,
USA, 1886

BELOW RIGHT:
Infiniti Red Bull Racing branding
Austria, 2005

authority. Most major newspapers have been augmented by digital editions to view on tablets, phones and computers, but these have been either abbreviations of the printed versions or simulations of their appearance. The *Guardian* has a highly sophisticated design identity and has developed a version of its daily news edition for all its digital platforms. Although it has similarities with the newspaper, such as the fonts, it is formulated to fit the screen and to incorporate interactive features and intuitive navigation, showing how graphic design can evolve an established brand to embrace new technologies on their own terms.

The earliest brand identities were the names of the products or their manufacturers, such as Coca-Cola and Heinz, but as consumers became more sophisticated a different type of visual language emerged, based on a more intuitive understanding of symbols. Shapes like the Nike "swoosh" or the numerous car marques that inevitably appear in virtually identical places on all car radiator grilles have been developed to be recognizable globally, regardless of the local language or alphabet. In Chapter 2 we saw how Barber Osgerby incorporated Olympic imagery, in the form of the linked ring logo, into the pierced surface of their relay torch. The first Macintosh computer, launched in 1984, bore only the Apple logo and not the brand's name, as have all its products ever since. This ensures relevancy and clarity in all the markets in which Apple operates. Apple is also the most valuable brand identity in the world; small wonder that it, and all corporate identities, are strenuously protected from imitators in the courts.

Brand logos originated in the very real, tangible world of foodstuffs and consumer goods, but as the virtual world has expanded it has not been immune to branding and corporate identity. Indeed, such is the potential value of "dot coms" and the fast-moving pace of competition in the realm of Internet trade that tech companies often fight hard to be the most recognizable brands. What is more, lacking tangible material values in their products and without the possibility of immersive experiences in retail stores, these brands rely on their corporate identities even more to distinguish themselves from competition.

ABOVE LEFT:
The Apple Store, London, is only identified by the Apple logo
2014

ABOVE RIGHT:
The Guardian digital edition
UK, 2014

Conventional wisdom is that a company's logo must be consistent even if it is tweaked and updated on occasion, but since 1998 Internet search-engine giant Google has been tampering with its own logo. A team of 10 "Google doodlers", both graphic designers and computer engineers, generate variations of the Google logo to appear on the site's homepage. These are tied to topical events or anniversaries, ranging from the frivolous to the seriously cultural. Sometimes they are even interactive games or puzzles. They may only appear for one day, but can take months to prepare. All the Google doodles are intended to humanize the highly-technical digital brand, as well as communicating it to global audiences through symbols rather than language.

Another side effect of the rise of the virtual world is the change in behaviour and attitudes it engenders in people. For example, social media like Facebook and Twitter encourage each of us to broadcast our life events and thoughts in ways similar to how brands advertise their values. Indeed, each of us is pressured to think of our own distinguishing brand identities, which may in fact derive from a portfolio of established brands that we like. This, combined with the rise of media-driven celebrity culture, inevitably leads to individual people becoming corporate identities. Kate Moss, for example, has a brand logo designed around her identity as a supermodel to distinguish and identify the fashion lines sold in her name by Topshop and perfumes bearing her endorsement.

Earlier in the book we saw how Barack Obama's image became a powerful tool in his first presidential campaign (see What is Design? on page 12). Political parties and presidents can be branded just like products and services, because they embody sets of values and promises and are seeking loyalty from the public, whether that is expressed through votes or through purchases. Obama's campaign team for the 2008 presidential race worked with Chicago advertising agencies to devise a logo that would represent the candidate and what he stood for. The circular shape evokes the initial of Obama's name while the red stripes and colour blue recall the stars and stripes flag. The logo also suggests the sun rising over the American plains. Put together, these elements powerfully promise a new day in American politics.

FAR LEFT:
Kate Moss logo
Designed by Peter Saville and Paul Barnes, UK, 2007

LEFT:
Barack Obama official election campaign logo
Designed by Sender LLC and mo/de, USA, 2008

A BUS FOR LONDON

The familiar red double-decker bus has become synonymous with London, a globally recognized symbol of the city. Its form has evolved over more than a century and was shaped by the needs of a rapidly expanding metropolitan public and the demands of an integrated transport network to serve it.

In the late nineteenth century London was booming and private operators began to provide horse-drawn omnibus services. These early buses evolved from stagecoaches, designed for longer cross-country journeys, and were limited in size by the capacity of the horses. Nevertheless, double-decker buses were in service on London's streets by the 1870s.

In 1910 the London General Omnibus Company introduced the B-type bus, the first mass-produced double-decker motorbus in service. By replacing the horses with engines, operators could massively enlarge the bus system and many new routes appeared servicing the expanding suburbs. About 2,500 of these B-type buses were built and many were shipped overseas to support military campaigns during the First World War.

During the 1920s and 1930s the London bus system was not fully regulated and routes proliferated, with many private companies in competition. At this time the upper deck could not be roofed because it would raise the centre of gravity and make the bus unstable. It was not until 1924 that the first bus with a lowered chassis appeared, allowing the exposed upper deck to be enclosed. Gradually, buses were becoming more recognizable as the vehicles we know today.

The entire system was amalgamated as London Transport in 1933 and the

LEFT:
Knifeboard horse-drawn omnibus
Trafalgar Square, London,
about 1870

authorities very quickly determined to standardize not only the design of the buses, to ease maintenance, but the livery of the bus services too. Just weeks before the outbreak of the Second World War, London Transport introduced the RT1 bus, the first we would recognize as the iconic London bus, with an enclosed roof and an open rear entrance platform for passengers. Like the coachman of its horse-drawn predecessors, the driver in his cabin was separated from the passengers, while a conductor collected fares and inspected tickets.

The war curtailed production of the RT1 but the form of the bus became the blueprint for the great Routemaster buses that followed it, prototyped from 1954 and in full service throughout London by 1959. We may think of the Routemaster as the iconic London bus, but in fact it represented the end of a long development. Over 7,000 examples were built and perhaps its status arises from its numerousness and longevity: the buses only left service in 2005, and a few remain on so-called "heritage routes" in central London.

The heyday of the Routemaster was in the 1960s, and buses were celebrated on film and television; Cliff Richard drove an RT bus in *Summer Holiday* in 1963 and the sitcom *On the Buses*, aired between 1969 and 1973, featured another precursor to the Routemaster, the Bristol Lodekka. Both demonstrate how buses had entered British popular culture. But at the same time social and economic challenges were bringing about radical changes to bus design. London Transport needed to cut costs and could achieve this by removing conductors from buses. Redesigned as "one-man operated" vehicles, new buses from the 1970s had front entrances rather than open rear platforms, enabling the driver to collect fares. Their boxy frames contrasted with the more streamline Routemasters and their antecedents that showed the influence of 1930s "moderne" styling.

Other considerations were coming into play too, for example, convenience and

ABOVE LEFT:
AEC Regent III bus – RT1
1939

ABOVE RIGHT:
The first Routemaster bus in service
Crystal Palace, South London, February 1956

safety. The Disability Discrimination Act 1995 required all buses to be wheelchair accessible by 2000. Newer buses had more space for standing passengers and baby-buggies, adjustable suspension to allow them to lower at bus stops to aid access, and retractable ramps for wheelchairs. None of this was possible on the Routemasters. Increasingly, the convenience of hopping on and off the open platform of the Routemaster was regarded as a public-safety liability. Despite its popularity, the days of the Routemaster were numbered.

So-called "Bendy Buses" appeared in London in 2001. These long single-deckers could accommodate more passengers than double-deckers and the central articulation enabled them to take tight corners. Their introduction coincided with an increase in the popularity of urban cycling and the congestion charge imposed on private vehicles in central London. Bendy-buses were behemoths, unloved by motorists jostling for road space and loathed by cyclists after a number of fatalities. Now, the original Routemasters seemed almost petit and nippy through urban traffic. In his mayoral campaign in 2008, Boris Johnson exploited Londoners' fondness for the Routemaster and vowed to eliminate bendy-buses in favour of a new style of the iconic London double-decker: by 2011 the last articulated buses had been withdrawn.

A competition to design a new bus for London was launched by Transport for London in July 2008. This was a complicated affair, requesting general ideas or concepts for a whole new bus or details that could be incorporated into a new design. The winning designs, which included a glass-roofed bus designed by Foster + Partners, were passed to manufacturers for tendering in late 2008. By May 2009, Northern Irish manufacturer Wrightbus had won the tender to build 600 buses over three years. These would accommodate 87 passengers, have a closable rear platform, a flat lower floor to aid access, and a hybrid fuel system to reduce pollution. The styling was contributed by Heatherwick Studio, the designers of the UK Pavilion at the Shanghai World Expo in 2010 and the Olympic cauldron at the London 2012 Olympic Games.

ABOVE & LEFT:
LT2 bus
Designed by Heatherwick Studio,
Manufactured by Wrightbus, UK, 2012

The appearance of the new "Bus for London" owes much to the legacy of the old Routemasters but is also shaped by the needs of a modern city. It is larger, more comfortable, has improved lighting and heating, is accessible to all and is more efficient than previous buses while still having a distinctive identity and association with the "design DNA" of previous models. For example, the moquette seat covers have been redesigned and the all-important rear platform retained, which can be closed during quiet periods to enable the bus to be operated solely by the driver. Unlike any previous double-decker bus, it has three entrances and two staircases. The interior is characterized by striated panelling, repeated layered forms are a Heatherwick Studio characteristic, for example, the interior of the Longchamp stores in New York, and externally the sweeping diagonal stair windows make the buses instantly recognizable on the London streets. The first prototypes entered service in February 2012, with all 600 buses promised to be in service by 2016.

LEFT:
LT2 bus, interior
Designed by
Heatherwick Studio
Manufactured by Wrightbus,
UK, 2012

OPPOSITE:
Longchamp store,
New York City, interior
Designed by
Heatherwick Studio,
UK, 2004

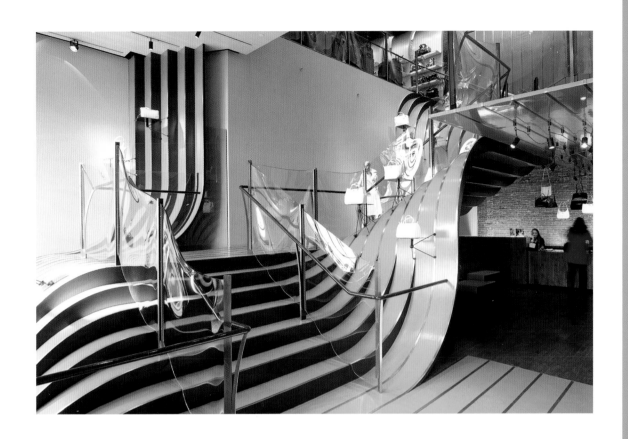

TASK CHAIRS

The familiar office chair, or task chair, is a strange hybrid piece of furniture. Perhaps more than any other chair (apart from reclining chairs in dental surgeries), it is designed as a piece of equipment, or a tool. Its purpose as a comfortable and suitable seat for conducting desk work reflects the ways in which modern ideas of the working week have shaped our world and our individual behaviour over the last century and a half. They are also the most technically advanced items of furniture in terms of material innovation and the most industrial in terms of how they are made.

Until the mid-nineteenth century most offices were small, and were likely to be furnished with utilitarian, all-purpose wooden chairs. The Industrial Revolution, which had greatly increased production of goods, inspired a revolution in trade and business too, and "white collar" clerical workers began to proliferate in Europe and North America. Offices expanded in size and number and, as we have seen previously with the introduction of the innovative paper clip, designers addressed the new conditions of office life.

The archetypal form of the task chair appeared quite quickly but no single chair or designer can claim all the innovations. The emphasis was on increasing comfort for desk-workers by making chairs adjustable and adding motion to them. In the 1840s and 1850s tilting mechanisms were introduced, possibly inspired by

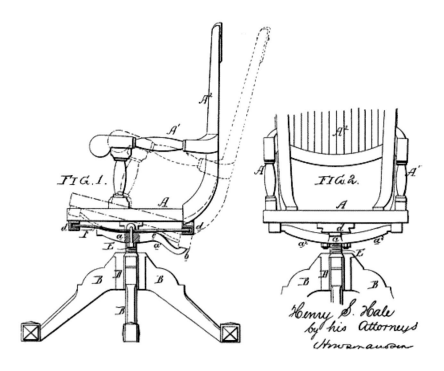

LEFT:
Patent drawing for a tilting chair
Designed by Henry S. Hale,
USA, 1875

rocking chairs. At the same time, chairs were designed with rotating bases to give them flexibility: swivel bases did away with conventional legs at the corners and introduced the idea of a central stem or pedestal, still a defining feature of how task chairs look today. The stem was rooted in a heavy cast iron platform at floor level, giving the chair weight and stability. Over time the platform gradually evolved into a star-shaped base to maintain its spread but reduce its mass. A few mid-twentieth-century chairs had three-legged bases but these are inherently unstable and are now banned. Four-legged bases have now largely been superseded by five-legged versions that provide optimum stability. Castors and glides have been a feature of task chairs ever since the naturalist Charles Darwin made his own contribution to their development by adding wheeled bed legs to his chair in the 1840s to make it easier for him to move around his study. By the end of the nineteenth century the characteristics of task chairs were in place: they should be adjustable, they should incorporate movement mechanisms and they should be mobile.

Twentieth-century task chair design was principally a refinement of these characteristics. The manufacture of task chairs became increasingly industrialized, particularly after the Second World War when innovations such as heavy-duty glues, compound-moulded plywood and fiberglass, which had been developed for military use, found their way into peacetime factories. Nineteenth-century chairs were very heavy, made of wood and cast iron. Designers in the twentieth century experimented with lighter substitutes such as die-cast aluminium and, from the 1960s, plastics.

ABOVE LEFT:
Aluminium Group chair
Designed by Charles and Ray Eames, Manufactured by Herman Miller, USA and Vitra, Switzerland, 1958

ABOVE RIGHT:
Synthesis 45 chair
Designed by Ettore Sottsass, Manufactured by Olivetti, Italy, 1973

In the past chairs were made by hand or semi-industrially in batches, but the introduction of new materials and expensive processes such as injection moulding transformed the sector. It was simply unaffordable for small firms to invest in the tooling and machinery, and task chair production came to be dominated by a small number of mostly American manufacturers, such as Steelcase, Herman Miller and Knoll, and in Europe by Vitra and Wilkhahn. As late as the 1950s, the architect Frank Lloyd Wright was able to design an office building and the chairs to go in it, but this era of bespoke office furniture has largely passed.

In 1911 Frederick Winslow Taylor published *The Principles of Scientific Management* in which he separated workers according to specialism and in a hierarchy of seniority. "Taylorism" became the guiding principle for the organization of twentieth-century workplaces and influenced design of task chairs. Until the 1990s, ranges of office chairs commonly would have up to five variants reflecting the hierarchy of different users, usually indicated through size and materials. An executive would sit in a much larger and plusher chair than his secretary, for instance. Although the characteristics of task chairs arose for reasons of functionality and efficiency, the chairs also had symbolic values. Perhaps it is

BELOW:
Aeron chair
Designed by Bill Stumpf
and Donald Chadwick,
Manufactured by Herman Miller,
USA, 1994

OPPOSITE:
Liberty chair
Designed by Niels Diffrient,
Manufactured by Humanscale,
USA, 2002

for this reason that executives' chairs tended to evoke leather-clad library chairs while the seats used by ordinary clerical workers were upholstered in everyday textiles. Aside from design aberrations that coupled reproduction antique-style chairs with swivel bases, task chair designs have celebrated their engineering, their use of advanced materials, and their futuristic, even space-age modern aesthetic – presumably to signal the power and primacy of the corporate clients that purchased them.

What is the appeal of designing a task chair? The sector is very crowded already and the archetypal form is very fixed. Perhaps the attraction to designers is the ubiquity of task chairs and their intimate relationship with the human body: they present an ongoing challenge to get right. Initially office chairs were designed to increase the comfort, and with it the productivity, of clerical workers. From the 1980s onwards, as computers became more and more commonplace in all aspects of office life, it was not only their comfort but also their safety that became paramount. Metaphorically tied to their keyboards for eight hours a day, office workers were liable to strain their backs, necks and wrists unless they were properly supported. Task chair design became increasingly obsessed with ergonomics and designers, including Niels Diffrient and Bill Stumpf, vied to design evermore refined adjustability mechanisms. The Aeron chair, designed by Stumpf and Donald Chadwick in 1994, claimed to be the first chair to address the specific needs of a computer user. It also abandoned the old hierarchical symbolism of chairs, and was simply offered in three sizes entirely dependent on the size of the sitter, not their corporate status.

The checklist of adjustable features for task chairs keeps growing as technical innovations appear. Seat height adjustment was revolutionized by the introduction of the pneumatic gas strut in 1970 and today the depth of seats can be altered too. Armrests can be raised and lowered, and on some chairs the arms can be widened to accommodate larger people. Chair backs often incorporate adjustable lumber supports, or have self-adjusting headrests to keep the head vertical even when the chair back is reclined. The Aeron chair is typical of many task chairs that make much of their high-tech engineering and seem more like futuristic pieces of scientific equipment than mere typing chairs. In a sense, the old hierarchical symbolism continues, and chairs like this suggest the cut and thrust of the international bankers and corporate lawyers who occupy them.

Having mastered how to support every limb of an office worker at a computer, the trend today is for chairs to respond to different seating postures and use conditions. The IT revolution that drove task chair design since the 1980s has itself moved on; computers are now smaller and the digital realm can be accessed anywhere, not just at a desk. Chairs, like the Generation range launched by Knoll in 2009, are now designed to accommodate numerous formal and relaxed postures as a response to workplace trends that are more about team dynamics and interaction and less about individuals facing their screens. Oddities like Konstantin Grcic's 360° try to redefine the paradigm of task seating altogether.

BELOW:
360°
Designed by Konstantin Grcic,
Manufactured by Magis,
Italy, 2009

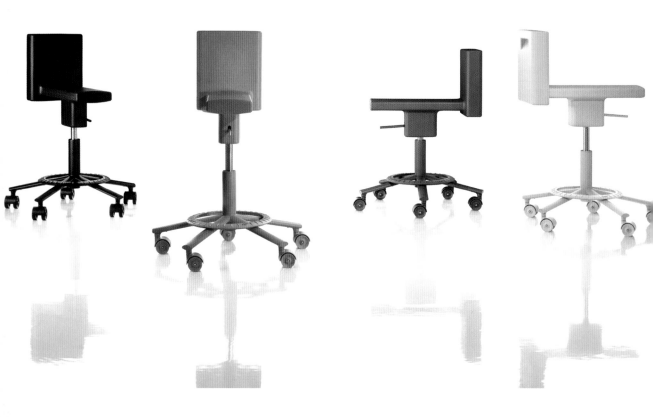

Task chairs developed because modern office-bound workers required them. They have been the focus of material and technical innovations and symbolically defined how status amongst workers was perceived. The transformation of work wrought by the digital revolution also transformed work chairs into precision ergonomic equipment. The changing reality of work will continue to influence task chair design, as the challenge to make more sustainable office furniture has already transformed the sector. The next challenge is the dissolving office environment itself. Increasing numbers of us are homeworkers (some 40 per cent of computer giant IBM's workforce work at home) and the needs of the home office will dictate how task chairs evolve from this point.

ABOVE:
Generation range of task chairs
Designed by Formway, Manufactured by Knoll, USA, 2009

SUSTAINABLE TASK CHAIRS

Since many millions of task chairs are produced annually, manufacturers are rightly focused on sustainable production issues, trying to limit polluting manufacturing processes and materials. This includes designing chairs to be dismantled easily to aid replacement of worn or broken parts and recycling. An early instance was Wilkhahn's Picto chair, designed in 1991, which featured separable components to aid repair and recycling. One of the first chairs to be marketed as sustainable was Herman Miller's Mirra chair, designed by Studio 7.5 in 2003. The manufacturer claimed the chair contained 42 per cent recycled materials. Glen Oliver Löw designed the Think chair for Steelcase in 2004 (updated in 2014) with a focus on simplifying the number of components and the possibility of recycling materials.

LEFT:
Think chair
Designed by Glen Oliver Löw,
Manufactured by Steelcase,
USA, 2004 (updated 2014)

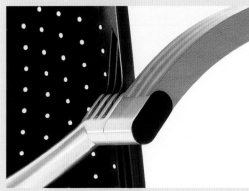

ABOVE:
Mirra chair
Designed by Studio 7.5,
Manufactured by Herman Miller,
USA, 2003

ABOVE:
Picto chair and detail
Designed by ProduktEntwicklung Roericht,
Manufactured by Wilkhahn, Germany, 1991

GAMING

Until the 1970s games where players could control the action taking place on video screens were restricted to arcades. These arcade games were large-scale, expensive booths that had developed from the bagatelles and pinball machines that had populated seaside arcades and fairs since the middle of the twentieth century. The advent of computing rapidly found a commercial application in gaming, and it is reasonable to give credit to the video game industry for being a driving force behind the advancement of computing itself. In this section we will look at both the development of the games themselves and at the design of the controllers and consoles that delivered them into the hands of eager consumers, since both are interdependent.

ABOVE:
Pong games console
Manufactured by Atari, USA, 1975

The first commercially available gaming console for the home was Magnavox's Odysset, launched in 1972. It was, however, Atari's launch of the Pong console three years later that really saw home-gaming take off. *Pong* was a tennis-inspired game for two players and, like many subsequent consoles, it could be attached to a television set. It featured just two rotating knobs, one for each player, to control the motion of the on-screen "players", which were nothing more than oblong cursors between which a square "ball" could be batted at varying speeds. 1970s games consoles could play only single games and were not the versatile machines that developed later. The games themselves were developed by individuals, or perhaps very small teams of programmers, in a matter of weeks. By 1977 Atari had developed a console capable of operating multiple games supplied on cartridges. Atari's consoles were extremely popular and introduced classic games such as *Space Invaders* (first released in 1978 for arcades, and in 1980 for home consoles). The two-dimensional, pixelated graphics typify their era and were the result of limited computing power. The games industry in the 1980s was experimental, fast-growing and hard-fought, as both the market for games and the computing power to support them grew exponentially. Many smaller companies that were active then have since vanished.

LEFT:
Space Invaders computer game
Published by Atari, USA, 1978

ABOVE:
2600 games console
Manufactured by Atari, USA, 1977

In 1985 Nintendo, originally a Japanese maker of playing cards, entered the market with its Entertainment System console, featuring an independent, handheld controller. The controller had buttons of various shapes, including a cross to control vertical and lateral movements on screen. Nintendo enjoyed enormous success with games it developed itself, most notably *Super Mario Bros.*, but games by third-party developers could also be played on the consoles. The company consolidated its position with the first handheld games console to have its own screen, the Game Boy, in 1989 and with games like *Tetris* to play on it.

The early 1990s were characterized by the battle for supremacy between Nintendo and Sega, with its famous *Sonic the Hedgehog* game (1991), and computing power increased from 16-bit to 32-bit and ultimately to 128-bit consoles. Sony entered the market in 1994 with the PlayStation console, a 32-bit machine with a single controller to be held in both hands. Controllers at this time looked similar and were largely designed to be ergonomic, allowing players to use their fingers and thumbs to control action through various buttons. The PlayStation's buttons featured triangular, square, cross-shaped and circular symbols, giving birth to a new symbolic language in gaming that transcended any conventional alphabets.

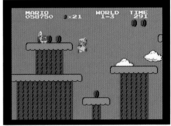

LEFT:
Entertainment System games console
Manufactured by Nintendo, Japan, 1985

ABOVE:
Super Mario Bros. computer game
Published by Nintendo, Japan, 1985

Another innovation of the PlayStation was that games with realistic 3D perspective could be played. Increasingly the quest for realism became the major goal for games developers. A landmark in this respect was a driving game called *Indianapolis 500: The Simulation* that was launched for personal computers (which had more computer power than consoles) in 1989. The PlayStation received a great boost from the realism of the first *Gran Turismo* driving game in 1998. At this time, a car in the game was modelled from about 400 "polygons", the building blocks from which all elements of computer game graphics are constructed and would take about a day to programme. Only 10 years later, a car would take six months to build and comprise some 40,000 polygons. This is because new software with shader techniques and texture maps increased the realism of the car, right down to the build-up of dirt on a windscreen and the way the windows caught the light from a virtual sunset. Realism within the virtual gaming world increasingly aspired to be cinematic. Games like *Gran Turismo*, with increased attention to detail in the look and feel of the gaming environment, took teams of 20 programmers about a year to develop as the industry began to mature.

By the late 1990s gaming was firmly embedded in popular culture, as witnessed by the phenomenal success of the *Tomb Raider* series (launched in 1996), which featured the indomitable Lara Croft, a rare female action hero, and (unlikely as it may seem) an English aristocrat. Subsequently expanding into comic books, novels, theme park rides and even movies (two film versions cast Angelina Jolie as Lara Croft), as well as at least 11 generations of the game itself, *Tomb Raider* demonstrates the flexibility and reach that is possible for computer games.

In 2001 Microsoft, the last major brand to enter the market, launched the Xbox. By using technology drawn from the PC industry, the Xbox achieved greater performance than its biggest rivals, Nintendo and Sony, and since then these three companies have dominated gaming.

ABOVE:
PlayStation games console
Manufactured by Sony, Japan, 1994

ABOVE RIGHT:
Gran Turismo computer game
Developed by Polyphony,
Published by Sony Computer
Entertainment, Japan, 1998

RIGHT:
Gran Turismo 5 computer game
Developed by Polyphony Digital Inc.,
Published by Sony Computer
Entertainment, Japan, 2008

Computing power has made game graphics almost realistic, but consoles and other gaming equipment have appealed to our other senses to give players a sense that their experiences are real. Plug-in equipment like steering wheels and pedal sets give driving-game players real-time force feedback vibrations that simulate driving real cars. For some time, joystick and handheld controllers had included rudimentary vibrating "rumble" technology to suggest feedback, but the first compelling force feedback came with the steering wheel supplied for *Gran Turismo 3* on the PlayStation 2 in 2001. Compact discs superseded cartridges for storing games and their larger memories allowed games developers to include more sophisticated soundtracks. The music and other noises were not just atmospheric, but could also be the source of sensory feedback for players. As budgets climbed into millions of dollars per game, developers could record actual racing cars to add their sounds to racing games. Verisimilitude was further enhanced by using data from car manufacturers to set the performance parameters and design details of vehicles represented in games. The Xbox 360, launched in 2005, introduced full perspective immersive graphics in all directions, a far cry from the top-down, two-dimensional pixelated graphics of the earliest consoles.

The last major paradigm shift in gaming was brought about by the launch of the Nintendo Wii in 2006, which introduced motion sensors into the wireless controllers. For decades gaming had largely been a sedentary, or at least a seated, activity, but the Wii allowed players to interact with games much more physically. The motion sensor technology was well suited to games that simulated sports such as golf and tennis. In response, both Xbox and PlayStation introduced their own motion-sensor controllers too.

Today the teams developing new games include hundreds of personnel, with many programmers and artists as well as legal, licensing and marketing teams, and budgets more like those for Hollywood movies than the cottage industry from which gaming has grown. Gamers demand immersive experiences so developers go to great lengths to deliver it. For example, the makers of *Race Driver: GRID* (2008), set at the famous Le Mans racetrack, photographed the entire 13.6km track and every feature that would be visible to the drivers to simulate in their

LEFT:
Xbox games console
Manufactured by Microsoft,
USA, 2001

game, including a 30,000-strong crowd of spectators. Game design is a major international industry and one in which Britain excels, notably with Rockstar North in Edinburgh, the studio behind the *Grand Theft Auto* series of games. In 2013, *Grand Theft Auto V* broke all records by achieving sales of $1 billion in just three days from its launch. Viewed like this, video games, which began so unassumingly with *Pong* over 40 years ago, now rival the mightiest sector of the entertainment industry, Hollywood itself.

It is ironic that games have sought to render virtual worlds more realistically, increasingly becoming visually more cinematic and more physically tactile in the ways they are controlled. Virtual worlds are not bound to follow the laws of nature or physics, yet these are the parameters many games developers have set for themselves. A second irony lies in the way in which the movie industry uses very similar software technology to create believable renderings of impossible worlds, such as *Avatar*, or to depict the attributes of superheroes, whereas gaming seems set on simulating the real world, or at least a very heightened impression of it. The real and the virtual worlds are set to converge in ever more puzzling and dramatic ways once augmented reality technology really takes off, discussed in more depth in the next chapter. Already Google Glass and the Oculus Rift headset designed for gaming have taken enormous strides in this direction. Microsoft's Kinect for the Xbox 360 console can be controlled by voice command or motion and can detect the room in 3D. It may have been developed for entertainment but it has great potential in other areas, such as surgical applications. Microsoft recognizes this and has issued a software development kit to allow professionals to develop such applications: in a sense it marks the moment gaming and the real world became truly aligned.

ABOVE LEFT:
Wii games console
Manufactured by Nintendo, Japan, 2006

ABOVE RIGHT:
Players interacting with the motion sensor handset of a Wii games console

TRAINING SHOES

Sports training shoes – known more familiarly in the USA as sneakers and colloquially in the UK simply as trainers – purport to be the most highly technical and advanced footwear available. If, as I have already suggested, design is about problem solving and improving our ability to respond to the environment, then training shoes can be seen as a prime example of our attempts to become superhuman. Every one of them makes claims to improve our speed and agility.

The evolution of training shoes should be seen in the context of a fascination with sport and health dating from the early twentieth century; an interest partly the result of medical and dietary innovations that enabled people to lead healthier and more active lives than ever before. What is more, many people in the developed world had greater access to leisure time to pursue sport. Against this backdrop, the earliest shoes designed to improve the performance of athletes also had the benefit of material innovation, most notably the process of hardening rubber by "vulcanizing" it with sulphur at high temperatures. Vulcanization (see Chapter 6) made car tyres possible and revolutionized transport, and it made rubber shoe soles possible too, permitting for the first time the design of light, flexible and durable sports shoes. Several American shoes are claimed to be the first rubber-soled shoes. PRO-Keds, produced in 1917, were made by a firm that held a licence for vulcanization. Apart from a few reissues of classic designs the brand has largely disappeared. Better known are Converse All Star shoes which also first appeared in 1917 and are still made today. They are characterized by the simple pairing of canvas uppers with rubber soles. Marquis M. Converse founded his eponymous firm in 1908 and the brand was one of the first to realize the potential of endorsements by sportsmen, adding the name of prominent basketball player Chuck Taylor to their All Star shoes in 1923. Basketball remains one of the sports most associated with trainers.

The vast majority of technical innovations in athletic shoes have been concerned with cushioning impact, reducing the weight of the shoe, dissipating heat from the foot, and ensuring accuracy of fit. Plastics like EVA (ethylene vinyl acetate) and TPU (thermoplastic urethane) are used in "motion control" areas, that is to say the suspension and "bounce" areas. There are also proprietary technologies with terms like Air, Pump, Disc and Torsion. Nike is a relative newcomer to the training shoe world and has pioneered many technical innovations. Named after the Greek goddess of victory, and with a world famous "swoosh" logo, Nike emerged in Oregon in 1971 from a business that imported Japanese running shoes. The Air system first appeared in 1987 and variations persist to this day. Nike introduced pockets of air into its soles to cushion impact, and made transparent windows in the heels to reveal them. In 1989 Nike's Air Pressure shoes came with an air pump to adjust the pressure in chambers around the ankle support to perfect a custom fit (Reebok introduced a similar system in 1993). A further innovation in 2000 introduced the Nike Shox range, featuring PU foam columns in the heel that acted as shock absorbers.

ABOVE:
Waffle training shoes
Manufactured by Nike,
USA, 1974

OPPOSITE:
**Converse All-Star
training shoe**
Manufactured by Converse,
USA, Since 1917

Many Nike innovations have emulated barefoot running, for example the Nike Air Sock Racer in 1985, which was more like a tight-mesh sock than a shoe, and the Nike Air Rift 10 years later, which was inspired by Kenyan barefoot long-distance runners and was named after the Great Rift Valley where they train. One of the first shoes to have a cloven toe detail, the Air Rift was intended to simulate being barefoot as much as possible while retaining the benefits of a cushioned sole. The Nike Air Presto shoes, launched in 2000, were marketed like T-shirts and were similarly sized XS to XXL rather than with conventional shoe sizes. They featured a very lightweight, washable stretch-mesh upper.

American brands may dominate the training shoe sector but there are innovative European brands too. Adolf and Rudolf Dassler produced their first running shoes in Germany in 1920, and the American sprinter Jesse Owens wore Dassler shoes to win four gold medals at the Berlin Olympics in 1936. However, the brothers fell out and each set up his own brand, both of which survive to this day. Rudolf launched Puma in 1948 and Adolf combined his nickname with the first letters of his surname to create adidas, which launched the following year. Most of the evolutionary innovations of these well-known brands have been in the realm of marketing and styling their products, and realizing how sportswear could cross from the athletic track into the fashion mainstream. This is not to say they

OPPOSITE:
Air Max training shoes
Manufactured by Nike, USA,1987

BELOW:
Air Rift training shoes
Manufactured by Nike, USA, 1995

neglected designing for serious athletes – adidas has had a long relationship with the German national football team, for example, and the boxer Muhammad Ali – but that they gave attention to appearance as well as performance. In 1984 their products entered popular culture when rap legends Run-DMC wore classic adidas Superstar basketball shoes, which were first introduced in 1969. The band is also credited with introducing the fashion for wearing training shoes unlaced and with the tongue sticking out, still an urban fashion 30 years later.

While fashionable wearers of adidas sneakers may have determined not to use the laces, one of Puma's innovations was to do away with laces altogether. In 1994 it introduced the Disc system, a lace-less mechanism that allowed wearers to adjust the tightness of the fit. The system has not caught on and we still use laces in our trainers.

Shoes like Nike's Shox range celebrated the highly technical and engineered character of the shoes and simultaneously appeared to transform their wearers into androids. Another trend has been bio-mimicry, in which the shoes are inspired by nature rather than engineering. A good example is the Air Max 95, designed by Sergio Lozano for Nike. Each element of the shoe represents a different part of the

BELOW:
Air Presto training shoes
Manufactured by Nike,
USA, 2000

RIGHT:
Superstar training shoes
Manufactured by adidas,
Germany, 1969

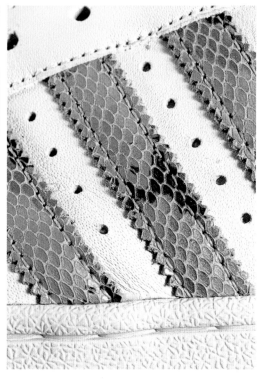

human body. The midsole (the section between the upper and the outsole) is like the spine, anchoring the rest of the features. From this grow graduated side panels like muscles, and the loopholes on their supports are like ribs. Finally the upper is encased in mesh, like skin. Whether or not this design approach actually improves performance is questionable.

Training shoe brands continue to innovate almost a century after the first recognizable sneakers appeared. Areas of particular activity include making uppers lighter and more breathable, and to this end both adidas and Nike have introduced 3D knitted shoes in recent years. Arguably Nike's flirtation with barefoot running was ahead of its time, but the brand has persisted and has had more success with its Free Flyknit shoes.

I have focused on how performance-enhancing features have evolved but it should be mentioned that the aesthetics of training shoes are also in constant flux, largely due to their fashionability. Cult brands like Feiyue, Saucony and A Bathing Ape are avidly collected, as are rare models and re-editions by the major manufacturers. Collaborations with fashion designers (such as the relationship of adidas with Yohji Yamamoto) and street artists maintain trainers' cutting edge fashion credibility.

ABOVE:
Disc training shoes
Manufactured by Puma,
Germany, 1994

RIGHT:
Air Max 95 training shoes
Designed by Sergio Lozano,
Manufactured by Nike,
USA, 1995

11. DESIGN & INNOVATION

I n the previous chapter we looked at how several design typologies have evolved, sometimes over the period of generations. Products that are familiar today have often developed gradually and incrementally, shaped by numerous small changes initiated by many designers but also inspired by advances in materials and technologies, or by the demands of the market. In this chapter we will look at the relationship between design and innovation and at some of those paradigm-shifting moments that changed the course of design at a stroke.

"Innovation" is a much over-used and misunderstood word (rather like "creativity" and, indeed, "design"). We think it means something to do with new thinking and novelty, but many of us find it hard to be more specific than that. *The Oxford English Dictionary* includes "the action of introducing a new product into the market", but most of us would agree that not every new product is innovative and there are many "also rans" and "lookalikes". More helpfully, the dictionary considers innovation to mean "a political revolution; a rebellion or insurrection" which gives the term much more bite. Another definition is "a change made in the nature or fashion of anything; something newly introduced; a novel practice, method, etc.". Innovative design, therefore, is the way in which designers solve problems by thinking "outside the box" to come up with radical, game-changing solutions. This can be on a large scale or a very small one, such as the ways in which, in Chapter 3, we saw Ron Arad completely rethink the archetypical adjustable desk light.

It is easy to fall into a trap of thinking that innovative design is the same as new, original styling or thinking up novelties. In fact, I would argue that innovation has very little to do with the *appearance* of the product, having much more to do with how a product has been intellectually conceived by its designers. What does this mean in practice? It means designers are able to ask those "What if?" questions

BELOW:
When Jim Comes to Paris hospitality tower
Designed by Matali Crasset,
Manufactured by Domeau
& Pérès, France, 1995

RIGHT:
Steve Jobs launching the iPhone
San Francisco, January, 2007

that may seem naive, childlike or plain silly, but which cut through the preconceived expectations we all have about what should and should not happen and bring genuinely fresh insight. The French designer Matali Crasset has built her design practice around asking "What if?" questions. "What if Jim comes to Paris to visit us?", she once asked herself. "We have very little space, where will he sleep?" In response she designed a space-saving spare bed that folded up lengthways to create a "hospitality tower" with a very small footprint when not in use. "What if Jim needs to get up very early, or he wants to read in bed?", she asked. So she designed an alarm clock and a lamp to hook on to the column. By imagining a particular scenario she identified a specific design problem and a unique, genuinely innovative solution. The look and feel of the hospitality tower (which Crasset called, quite logically, When Jim Comes to Paris) came quite late in the process, once she had mastered the context for the product and what it needed to do.

When Jim Comes to Paris clearly illustrates how problem-solving thinking can enable a designer to generate original ideas, but it is a small gesture in the bigger picture of paradigm-shifting product innovations. In order to think about this, let us consider the Apple iPhone, often regarded as one of the most innovative products of our age.

Just one designer's name is generally attributed to the iPhone, that of Jonathan Ive, Senior Vice President of Design at Apple, but with such a complex technological product, manufactured and distributed globally, it is plainly impossible for it to have been the work of one individual. Ive may have set the parameters and vision for the project, but one imagines armies of designers and engineers were involved in realizing his intentions. The first iPhone was unveiled by Steve Jobs, the head of Apple, at the Macworld Conference and Expo in San Francisco in January 2007, and was launched to an eager American public in June that year, and in Britain in November. A revised and improved iPhone 4 was announced in June 2010, followed by the iPhone 5 just a year later. The iPhone 6 was inevitable for Apple to maintain its competitive edge; it was launched in September 2014.

The innovation in the iPhone was not to think about how good a telephone would look with a bigger colour screen, or even to introduce touch screen technology that eliminated the need for keys and buttons (although these flourishes greatly add to the distinctiveness of the handset). No, the innovation came in thinking about the essential nature of our relationship with the product.

Mobile telephones are still relatively new products: the first models only appeared in the 1980s and were barely mobile. We have already seen the impact of greater computer power on the gaming industry (see Chapter 10), and the miniaturization of computers, together with the growth and reach of the Internet and the plethora of content it bears, have greatly shaped mobile telephony. Apple did not instigate the digital revolution, but it has been one of its chief champions and beneficiaries. Before the iPhone, digital technologies were already changing the early, clunky mobile telephones into lifestyle accessories. We could send brief SMS text messages rather than speaking on a call, and once digital cameras became embedded into phones we could send picture messages as well.

Apple's innovation was to realize that the iPhone is not a telephone at all (though it evidently can function as one): it is a portable computer, a personal portal to a vast and unfathomable digital realm which happens to also make phone calls. Apple had previously rethought how we interact with our computer screens, replacing scroll-down lists of unappealing, alienating computer code with accessible, humanizing icons and the same graphic interface was applied to the iPhone. Now navigation around the phone was as simple as touching an icon to launch a function. And for the first time a handset included completely integrated mobile Internet access, making it as easy to surf the web as to make a call or send a text message.

To reinforce our acceptance of the iPhone as a miniature computer, all Apple products, from large desk-top monitors through tablet computers and laptops to iPhones and the tiny iPod music players, share the same visual and material language. As much as possible they are merely screens held in milled-aluminium housings with minimal detailing, buttons or visual interference. They are sealed and homogeneous, giving no clue as to what is happening within them, or even a way to open them. In contrast with the "look at me" aesthetic of the first iMac, discussed in Chapter 4 (which, incidentally, gave users a peek at its mysterious workings through its translucent shell), now, almost perversely, Apple ensures its products stand out in the crowded consumer technology sector by designing them as much as possible to disappear. This reductive design approach to the hardware thrusts our screen-based interaction with the software to the forefront of our experience with the product. In a sense, the products have dematerialized into simple blocks that give no indication of their function or purpose until they are switched on. Sometimes it is not even possible to guess which is the right way up (which is not a problem since there is no right way up for devices like the iPhone and iPad which have self-adjusting screens). We can even see these blank slabs in some way as physical metaphors for how the digital age has dematerialized our world. Now, all information and data exists somewhere out there in the digital "cloud" and Apple products are styled as windows that give us access.

Apple supported the innovative handset by initiating a wave of third-party development of software applications to use on it, from games to maps and interactive tools, to music libraries and, well, pretty much anything that could be imagined. It gathered these together in the App Store function, accessible through the iPhone. The standardized handsets, therefore, became the hub of a vast network of activities that could be selected by individuals to customize their own telephones, at a stroke revolutionizing not only how mobile phones operated but also how we used them. Stroking, pinching, stretching and scrolling are all finger gestures required to operate the interface with Apple's touch screens, and we can see how Apple has designed these actions because they appear natural and intuitive, both humanizing and cementing our close relationship with cutting-edge digital technology. An indicator of just how innovative the iPhone has been is the numerous handsets launched by rivals with the aim of scuppering it, from the BlackBerry to the Samsung Galaxy and Sony's Xperia.

ABOVE:
Icons for applications on an iPhone

DYSON

Sir James Dyson is a well-known British entrepreneur and inventor who made his name with the cyclonic vacuum cleaner that bears his name. Vacuum cleaners revolutionized domestic cleaning and were made possible by the spread of electricity supply to homes in the early decades of the twentieth century. The machines used electric motors to drive fans that simply sucked air through a filter and trapped dirt in a disposable paper sack. However, the power of the suction was greatly diminished as the sack filled. Dyson's innovation was to re-imagine the cleaner's mechanism, and he took inspiration from the air-filtering systems used in factories and sawmills: large cone-shaped cyclones that spin the dust out of the air by centrifugal force. Dyson determined to miniaturize these cyclones to make domestic vacuum cleaners. However, a paradigm-shifting idea does not immediately realize itself as a resolved product, and Dyson turned to a conventional iterative process of testing and prototyping to perfect his cleaner. In total he claims to have made 5,127 prototypes to achieve the production-ready vacuum cleaner.

ABOVE:
Sir James Dyson making prototypes of the cyclonic vacuum cleaner

ABOVE:
AM06 desk fan, AM07 tower fan, AM08 pedestal fan
Designed and manufactured by Dyson, UK, 2009 (updated 2014)

The innovations of Apple begin with "What if?" questions ("What if we could all be connected to the virtual, digital world all the time, wherever we went?"), which are answered by the ingenuity of engineers and technicians and given shape and clarity by designers. The design-led consumer products firm founded by James Dyson works along similar lines, and alongside the range of cyclonic vacuum cleaners he has launched washing machines, hand dryers and bladeless fans, all sharing similarly game-changing reimaginings of technology. In government policy circles, in Britain and the USA, innovation like this arises from education focusing on science, technology, engineering and mathematics – the so-called STEM subjects. But as Dyson and Apple both amply demonstrate, STEM-thinking is not enough. What is needed is the added creativity of artists and designers who are capable of giving form and appeal to the logical and pragmatic worlds of science and technology: we must add the arts to the mix and should be stressing the need for STEAM, not STEM education.

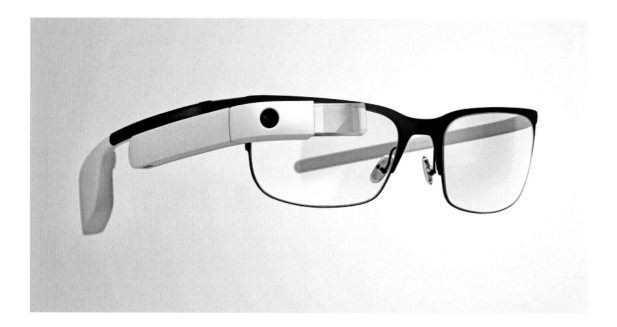

Given the hectic pace of technological change, the immeasurable gains to be made by those who control it and the competition amongst rivals, it is no wonder that digital technology brands pride themselves on innovative thinking. We have already seen how Google bucks trends with its own corporate identity, and it is no secret that a mark of success is when your brand name becomes a commonly understood verb (tens of millions of us "google" for information on the Internet every day). Google has mapped the entire world with satellite imagery and global positioning systems, and with its Google Glass headsets it aims to realise the science fiction dream of "augmented reality". Google Glass headsets are like spectacles with an additional clear lens on one side. This is a miniature screen that overlays the user's view of the natural world with a layer of digital information relating to it gleaned from the Internet. The conflation of virtual and actual worlds is what is meant by the term "augmented reality". As I have already suggested, Apple designs its hardware to be as invisible and neutral as possible: Google is going one step further, dissolving the computer into a wearable accessory for the body. If this seems worryingly like dystopian science fiction fantasies of people becoming androids and machines taking over the world, we need to regain our sense of perspective and remind ourselves that these are only consumer products. However, devices like Google Glass could play significant roles in military or terrorist activities, or crime in general, so perhaps we should bear in mind that applications of design innovation per se are not always benign.

ABOVE:
Google Glass headset
Designed and manufactured by Google, USA, 2013

RIGHT:
The Google Glass wearer's view of the world is augmented with an overlay of digital information

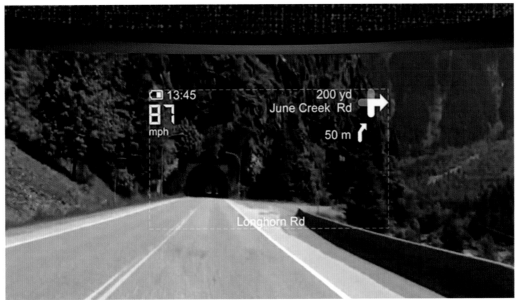

12. THE FUTURE OF DESIGN

Depending very much on your point of view, the future may seem either extremely bleak or exceptionally bright, but one thing is certain: it will be shaped, for better or worse, by design. In this book we have seen the many positive contributions design can make towards improving the quality of our lives, from tiny gestures to global solutions, but we have also seen design's role in destroying and polluting the planet. In this chapter we will look at some of the ways designers can affect the future, and how design-thinking itself can empower each of us to make a difference.

By the end of the twentieth century awareness of the environmental impact of our rampant consumer culture – fed by new products supplied by designers – was widespread. The old system of "take, make, waste" (that is, taking resources from the environment to make products that are rapidly disposed of) fuelled by a general acceptance of notions like "planned obsolescence" (see Chapter 4) was at last seen as unsustainable. In response, designers, manufacturers, retailers and – most importantly – consumers need to expect products to last longer than at present and to be repairable. Longevity is a key way in which resources can be better managed. Presently, most products are designed and made to maximize profit for the manufacturers at the point of sale, not really to provide enduring service (despite the promises suggested by "extended warranties"). We should expect much more of our products, especially technological and electrical devices that may contain thousands of components made of myriad materials, some rare or even dangerous. To design these to be disposed of in a few years is, on reflection, quite shameful, yet we are all complicit in the system of production and consumption that encourages this wastefulness. If consumers demand more longevity, we may find that our shoes and washing machines, cars and suitcases, smartphones and televisions cost more than they do now in the immediate term, but this will be because they are made to be more durable and are of better quality. In the longer term, a product that lasts twice as long as a short-lived rival should arguably cost half as much and certainly halves the environmental impact incurred by making a replacement.

But "built-in longevity" needs cooperation from many different parties, each with their own reasons to prefer the fast turnover of products in the market. An easier response to our anxiety about over-consumption has been the rise of individual and communal recycling schemes for our waste. Manufacturers and retailers have been compelled to redesign packaging to make it easier to recycle, or to be made of recycled materials. It is not just packaging, but the design of products that has been given attention: in an earlier chapter we saw how the makers of complex products such as task chairs responded by designing demountable, recyclable components (see Chapter 10). Perhaps these gestures made us feel less

SYMBOLIC RECYCLING

Bloomberg News is an international financial media company with the wherewithal to collect and process its own waste, largely comprising of vast quantities of computer monitors and cabling generated by the inevitable upgrading of information technology in its offices. Each year the independent curators Arts Co organize *Waste Not Want It*, a showcase exhibition in Bloomberg's European headquarters in London of bespoke furniture and installations by invited designers, all made using Bloomberg's own recycled waste. The results are often very inventive and beguiling, but can only make a symbolic contribution to the company's waste mountain, while raising awareness of sustainability issues amongst its workforce.

In future, projects like this need to lead to genuine reprocessing of discarded electrical and computer equipment, which in turn requires designers to consider the ultimate dismantling of their products at the design stage, and for economic and political provision to ensure it can happen.

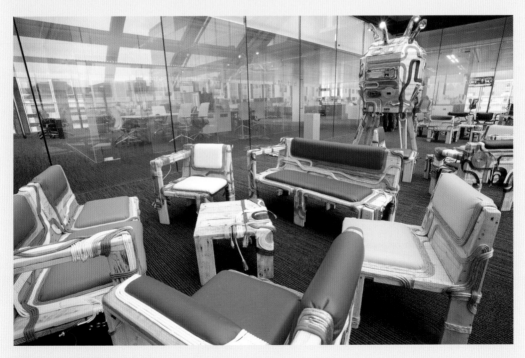

ABOVE:
RFIP furniture installation at Bloomberg News, London
Designed by Els Woldhek, UK, 2012

guilty, but the drive to recycle has done nothing to curb our consumption and may itself be fogging the issues.

This is because the vast majority of materials that are retrieved from the waste system are *downcycled*, which means they are recycled into lower grade materials or products, and the system merely interrupts their inevitable disposal. An influential book by Michael Braungart and William McDonough, published in 2002, confronted this system and has set the pace for many future design developments. In *Cradle to Cradle: Remaking the Way We Make Things* the authors challenged industry to design products that could be upcycled, meaning that the downward trajectory towards landfill, only temporarily interrupted by recycling, was reversed. Instead, McDonough and Braungart insisted that products should be designed in such a way that at the end of their useful life their components could become either "biological nutrients" (safe to re-enter the environment) or "technical nutrients" (capable of reuse by industry). "Cradle to cradle" thinking requires a major shift in the mindset of consumers and designers alike. It demands a much longer perspective than that which we are used to taking; rather than fixating upon our instant gratification through the purchase of products, we must take a longer view of the lifecycle of materials. We need to change our attitude from feeling that we are free to take resources from the natural world to one in which we are merely leasing those resources for a short period of time. Designers must focus on the end of their products' lives, not just the beginning.

How does "cradle to cradle" designing play out in practice? In the UK, the Royal Society of Arts is an institution dedicated to applying design thinking to enrich all of our lives. Under the stewardship of Sophie Thomas, the RSA's Co-Director of Design, it launched the Great Recovery programme in 2012, with the ambition of building a community of designers, scientists, manufacturers and recyclers to test "cradle to cradle" thinking. It will take time for these communities to make a lasting impact, but we can already see how individual designers have adopted the radical ideas of "cradle to cradle". The design partnership of Tristan Kopp (whose bicycle is included in Chapter 5) and Gaspard Tine-Beres is called Re-Do Studio. It works with local recycling schemes to recover discarded electrical kitchen appliances, such as toasters and kettles, which are disassembled to locate those components still in working order. Tine-Beres designed new kitchen appliances using standardized chemistry glass beakers, because of their uniformity and durability, and cork for the housings, because of its recyclability and its thermal and insulating qualities (illustrated in Chapter 5). The electrical components retrieved from discarded appliances are "technical nutrients", while the cork can be seen as a "biological nutrient" since it can re-enter the natural environment in due course without adverse consequences. The products are not only useful but propose a degree of social enterprise too, since the recycling and reassembling networks required to make them demand elements of skill and knowledge, at least at an amateur level, in order to make the products. Instead of being merely passive consumers, unaware of how our products are put together, the Re-Do products actively engage each of us.

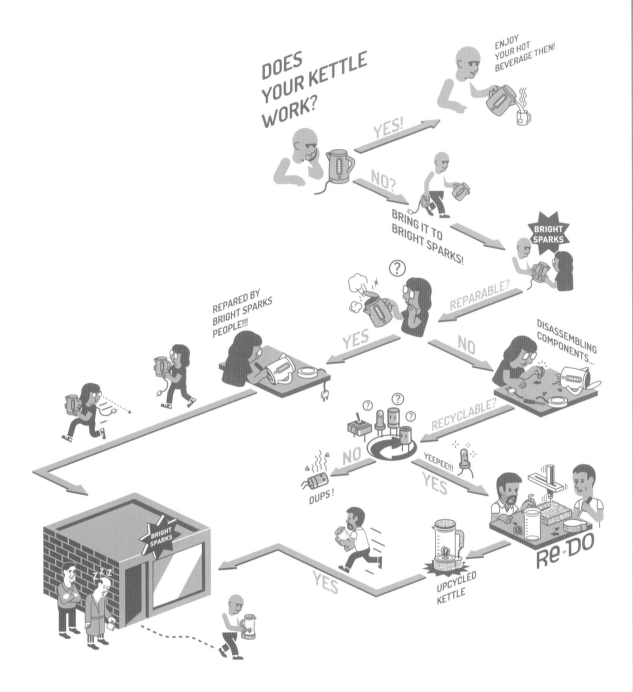

ABOVE:
Organizational diagram explaining the principles of upcycling
Illustration by Lou Rihn for Re-Do Studio, UK, 2012

Knowledge, skill and craftsmanship will give direction to design in the future, not just through the capabilities of professional designers, but because of design thinking's capacity to empower all of us. The sociologist Richard Sennett has written about the role of craftsmanship in contemporary society but he does not think only conventional crafts like ceramics or weaving need skill gained through practice. Anything, from playing a musical instrument to writing a book can be improved by gaining expertise, and expertise is skill learned through repetition and practice. Put another way, craftsmanship is the application of skill to solve problems. In design terms, this is analogous to the iterative and repetitious process of testing and prototyping in order to perfect a design. Sennett's view is important because it does not exclude anyone and promotes the idea that we all benefit from learning skills, just as Re-Do Studio's system requires people who have skills at disassembly and reassembly. Elsewhere in this book we have seen examples of "design as skill", for example Will Shannon and Joe Pipal's portable, personal factories described in Chapter 5. They both require a level of skill that can be learned by practice, but importantly they remain quite "lo-fi" design and manufacturing processes that empower just about anyone to make their own products. In a different way, Sugru (see Chapter 5) enables the customization of existing products, which is another way that consumers can become more engaged, more empowered and less passive.

BELOW:
Discarded electrical appliances: waste, or "technical nutrients"?

Sugru demonstrates the notion of hacking, which is the way in which we can all intervene in the conventional system of design and consumption that normally requires us to be simply passive recipients of one-size-fits-all, mass-manufactured products. Hacking is how we personalize and customize products, redesigning them to suit our individual requirements; in so doing, we gain making and design skills as well as a sense of empowerment and control. One instance is the way in which designers have chosen to regard international homeware giant Ikea not as a manufacturer of finished goods but as a supplier of components that can be reconfigured in numerous imaginative forms. Kieren Jones designed playful products like a sled by repurposing components of IKEA furniture.

FIXPERTS

The co-founder of Sugru, James Carrigan, is also the co-founder of Fixperts, together with independent curator and Professor of Design at Kingston University, Daniel Charny. Fixperts is not a company, but claims to be a "social project" and an "open knowledge-sharing platform". Throughout this book I have talked about design as a problem-solving exercise, and Fixperts promotes creative design solutions as ways of fixing problems. It is a combination of fixing and expertise, hacking systems, and mending and adapting products to make them work better, a kind of socially-oriented activism – or "hacktivism". Fixperts promotes the idea that design thinking should be taught in schools and colleges, not to breed a new generation of professional designers so much as to enable a generation of creative, independent individuals. By teaching the importance of collaboration and skill-sharing by producing films documenting design challenges, such as a teacher's attempts to mend the broken joy stick controlling the wheel chair of one of her students, Fixperts asserts design as an inclusive, beneficial, social and productive exercise. These aims are a far cry from our conventional understanding of design as the process of dressing up new products to make them more profitable.

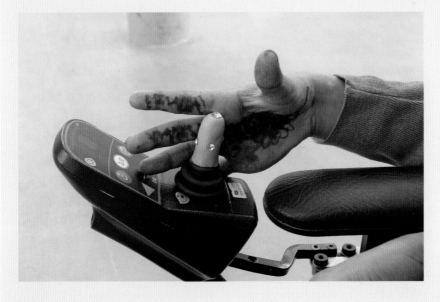

LEFT:
Film still from "A Chair for Foridha"
Produced by Fixperts, UK, 2012

ABOVE:
MakerBot Replicator 2X
Experimental 3D Printer,
Manufactured by MakerBot,
USA, 2012

The greatest advances in "design-as-empowerment" are happening as a result of the digital revolution. Whereas in the past advanced technologies were the exclusive preserve of the high-tech industries that controlled them, today computer-aided design software and hardware like 3D printers are becoming increasingly commonplace and available to all. This democratization of design tools is supported by innovations like Open Source design principles and Creative Commons licenses that circumvent the restrictions of copyright by giving everyone access to software and even specific designs by mutual agreement between designers and consumers. In Chapter 8 we saw many different applications that are being developed for 3D printing, from architecture to food. MakerBot is one of the best-known manufacturers of 3D printers and has inspired a community of technicians, engineers and designers with simple, low-cost machines capable of fabricating their own parts in order to build the next generation of printers. Self-reproducing robots may sound rather like the stuff of science fiction, but these machines make it possible for consumers and users of 3D printers to take control of their own hardware rather than purchasing a mass-produced product from an industrial supplier.

It is still small-scale and nascent, but the concepts behind MakerBot challenge conventional industrial design and manufacturing principles because they place expertise and skill in the hands of end-users. They promise to make it possible for each of us to design and print our own gadgets or components to repair existing products in our own homes. One application might be to print components from the Free Universal Construction Kit, a collection of 3D-printable connection modules, freely available from the Internet, that enable you to mix and match the 10 most popular children's construction toys, such as Lego and Duplo. In this

ABOVE:
**Kiosk 2.0 mobile
3D-printing facility**
Designed and made by
Unfold Design Studio,
Belgium, 2012

instance, design thinking has bridged a barrier created between the toy systems by the market and enabled freer play across all of them. Another possibility is for mobile units containing a computer, scanner and a 3D printer, such as Kiosk 2.0, that could provide services on street corners. To date, small 3D printers have been aimed largely at engineers and designers, but very quickly devices are appearing that have the look and feel of domestic equipment, like kitchen appliances, intentionally placing them in the domestic sphere. One of the first to offer professional-quality printing without the aesthetics of a robot or piece of workshop equipment is the Formlabs Form 1 3D printer. Will we soon have appliances like this in our home? And will they be useful?

In the space of a very short time the potential for everyone to be a digital designer and maker has become a reality. In part this was predicted and enabled by the work of Professor Neil Gershenfeld, Director of the Center for Bits and Atoms at the Massachusetts Institute of Technology (MIT), who published *Fab: The Coming Revolution on Your Desktop – From Personal Computers to Personal Fabrication* in 2005. Gershenfeld sees the potential for digital design and fabrication to design and produce local solutions to local problems. This perspective is quite at odds with the conventional view of design held since the Industrial Revolution, where design is a way to mass-manufacture identical design solutions to global problems. Taking the means of production out of the factory and into the hands of end-users represents a seismic shift in our understanding of the processes of design and consumption of products.

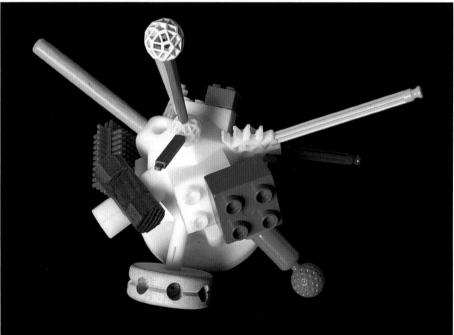

THESE PAGES:
Free Universal Construction Kit diagram,
components and constructed toy
Designed by Sy-Lab and The F.A.T. Lab,
USA, 2012

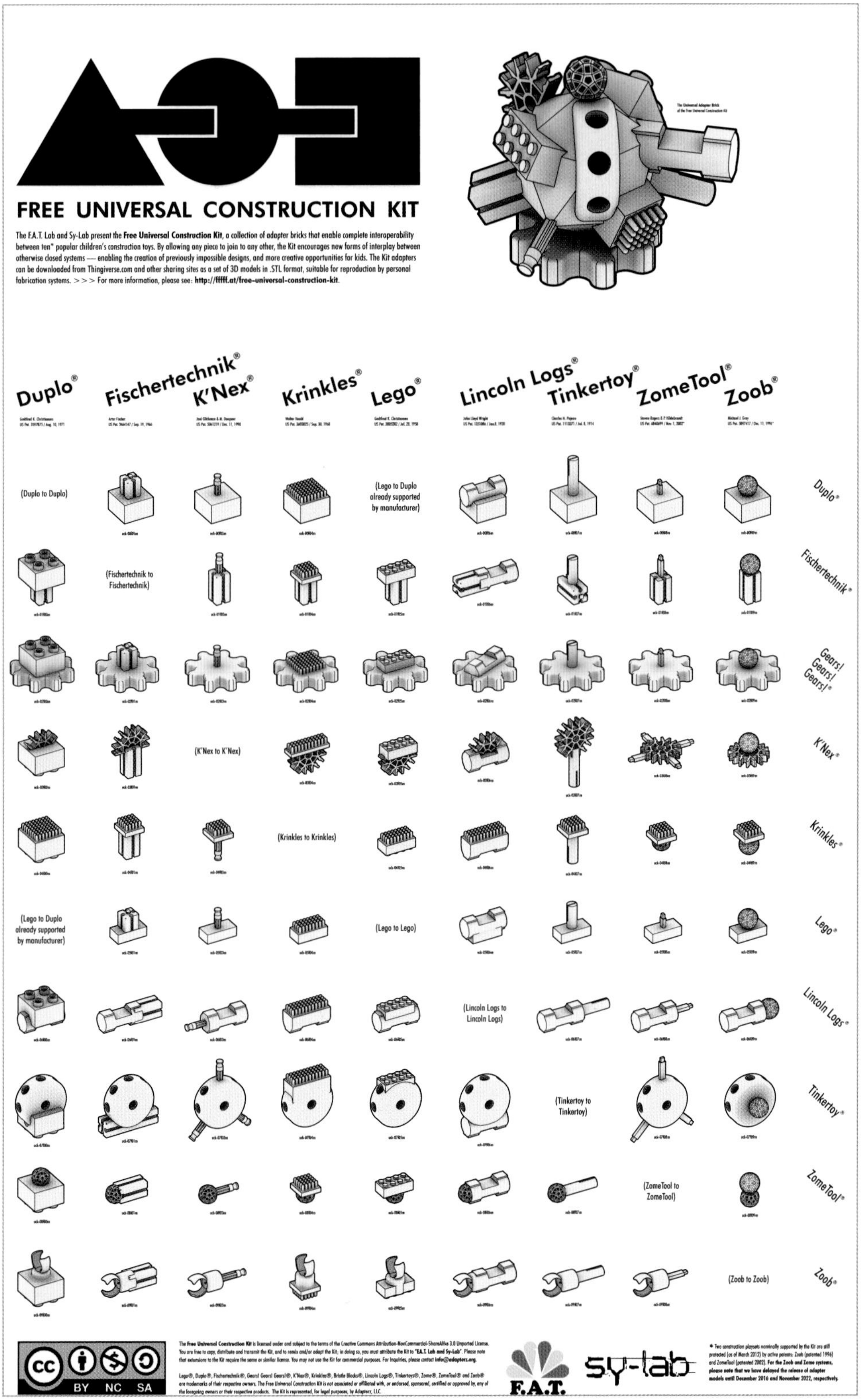
FREE UNIVERSAL CONSTRUCTION KIT
The F.A.T. Lab and Sy-Lab present the Free Universal Construction Kit, a collection of adapter bricks that enable complete interoperability between ten* popular children's construction toys. By allowing any piece to join to any other, the Kit encourages new forms of interplay between otherwise closed systems — enabling the creation of previously impossible designs, and more creative opportunities for kids. The Kit adapters can be downloaded from Thingiverse.com and other sharing sites as a set of 3D models in .STL format, suitable for reproduction by personal fabrication systems. >>> For more information, please see: http://fffff.at/free-universal-construction-kit.
Duplo®
Fischertechnik®
K'Nex®
Krinkles®
Lego®
Lincoln Logs®
Tinkertoy®
ZomeTool®
Zoob®
(Duplo to Duplo)
(Lego to Duplo already supported by manufacturer)
(Fischertechnik to Fischertechnik)
Gears! Gears! Gears!®
(K'Nex to K'Nex)
(Krinkles to Krinkles)
(Lego to Duplo already supported by manufacturer)
(Lego to Lego)
(Lincoln Logs to Lincoln Logs)
(Tinkertoy to Tinkertoy)
(ZomeTool to ZomeTool)
(Zoob to Zoob)
cc BY NC SA
The Free Universal Construction Kit is licensed under and subject to the terms of the Creative Commons Attribution-NonCommercial-ShareAlike 3.0 Unported License. You are free to copy, distribute and transmit the Kit, and to remix and/or adapt the Kit; in doing so, you must attribute the Kit to "F.A.T. Lab and Sy-Lab". Please note that extensions to the Kit require the same or similar license. You may not use the Kit for commercial purposes. For inquiries, please contact info@adapterz.org.
Lego®, Duplo®, Fischertechnik®, Gears! Gears! Gears!®, K'Nex®, Krinkles®, Bristle Blocks®, Lincoln Logs®, Tinkertoys®, Zome®, ZomeTool® and Zoob® are trademarks of their respective owners. The Free Universal Construction Kit is not associated or affiliated with, or endorsed, sponsored, certified or approved by, any of the foregoing owners or their respective products. The Kit is represented, for legal purposes, by Adapterz, LLC.
F.A.T.
sy-lab
* Two construction playsets nominally supported by the Kit are still protected (as of March 2012) by active patents: Zoob (patented 1996) and ZomeTool (patented 2002). For the Zoob and Zome systems, please note that we have delayed the release of adapter models until December 2016 and November 2022, respectively.

Gershenfeld's ideas inspired the foundation of Fab Labs (short for fabrication laboratories), specialist digital workshops supplying software and hardware to enable ideas to be turned into prototypes and products. There are now 200 Fab Labs in 40 countries; the first in Britain opening in Manchester (now there are nine in the UK, expected to rise to 30 in three years). Fab Labs give anyone access to cutting-edge technology and are particularly important for training the next generation of digitally-savvy young designers, people like Amy Mather, a 14-year-old Manchester schoolgirl whose work in the Fab Lab led her to design and make her own products and win the European Commission's first Digital Girl of the Year Award in 2013. Amy is not alone, and an army of self-motivated digital designer-makers is emerging, connected by Maker Faires and magazines such as *Make* that promote all forms of DIY and hacking design at the grass roots level.

ABOVE:
Form 1 3D printer
Designed and manufactured by
Formlabs, USA, 2013

RIGHT:
Make magazine
Published by Maker Media Inc.,
USA, since 2005

The future of design will largely reside in the hands of those with digital expertise and the ability to apply this to creative problem solving. Innovative ways to enable new design ideas to emerge will also play their part, such as crowd-sourcing financial backing through websites such as Kickstarter rather than relying on conventional sources of investment from banks. Indeed, specialist consultancies are already emerging to develop new ways of realizing design ideas, for example Sidekick Creatives, a London-based collective of designers, film-makers and media professionals who offer their services to individuals or companies who want to develop a product idea through crowd-sourcing financial backing.

WHY DESIGN MATTERS

In this book I have tried to unpack design and to explain why design is important, how designers think and test their ideas, and the contexts in which design takes place. I have included a little design history where it is helpful, such as the prevalence of modernist ideas in the twentieth century that are closely associated with shaping the look and feel of industrial products. We have looked at some of the prevailing factors in all design disciplines, for example the suitability of the form of the product to its function and purpose, and how designers can harness materials. Most of the book is about design today and tomorrow, about the challenges and constraints, but also the new opportunities facing designers.

As I have been writing I have become more and more firmly convinced that in design we have hope, as design is a positive, active, inclusive, collaborative process, building towards a shared vision of a better future … or at least it could be. Quite deliberately I have not written about "good" or "bad" design, which are subjective terms too closely entwined with individual taste and personal agendas. However, it should be clear from the selection of examples that, for me, worthwhile design should embrace those values I just listed, and that I have less interest or belief in design that sets up borders or is exclusive for the sake of it. And while trained, professional designers are essential in all disciplines, design thinking, which is active problem solving through an iterative, tested, creative process, is something we can all, and should all, take part in: design is for everyone, and everyone to some extent is a designer.

SO, WHY DOES DESIGN MATTER?

Design matters because we live in a world entirely shaped by humankind for our own benefit. Vast civil engineering projects, such as dams, ports and transport networks are design at a macro level, almost too large for us to comprehend because we can seldom see their parameters. The comforts we enjoy in the First World, and to which the developing nations quite reasonably aspire, are the fruits of managed and designed economic progress. At the same time, design has contributed to the over-exploitation of Earth's resources in our interests, but creative design-thinking can also help arrest our self-interest to gain back a natural balance that we have lost.

Design matters because since 1970 the global population has doubled. Now there are over seven billion people competing for resources; by the end of the century there will be 11 billion. Design can contribute real solutions to providing food, housing, medicine, transport and education that will sustain a booming population. More than this, design can be an agent by which global populations

ABOVE:
Minimal footprint living space
Designed by Solidspace,
UK, since 2003

maintain freedom, independence and human dignity. This happens on a global scale, but also very locally; consider, for example, innovative proposals for space-saving apartment blocks in crowded cities like London that face severe housing shortages.

Design matters because we desperately need alternatives to our over-reliance on fossil fuels. Designers can contribute by applying creative thinking to seek other means to power our world and fresh, sustainable sources of materials. Markus Kayser's solar sintering device (see Chapter 6) and Marjan Van Aubel's Current table that collects and stores solar energy both suggest new directions that exploit nature but do not corrupt it.

Design matters because designers can solve problems, both small and big, from packaging sandwiches to exploring deep space.

Design matters because scientists and engineers continually discover new materials, like Graphene (see Chapter 6), or reimagine the capability of computers.

Their innovations need designers to give them shape and purpose.

Design matters because it sits between the individualism of artistic expression and the logic of science and technology. Design takes from both and brings its own optimism and vitality to improve the world for everyone.

Design matters because it brings beauty and joy, like the Comedy Carpet that celebrates the catchphrases of famous comedians in granite and concrete typography set into Blackpool's well-known promenade.

Design matters because it gives each of us our independence and helps us to express our individuality. Design empowers us to make our own choices and to think for ourselves.

Design matters because it is political. It can be an agent of change. The Café of Equivalent$ was a pop-up event in the heart of the City of London that offered lunch to financial workers, priced at the equivalent percentage of income that a person in the developing country would have to spend on a meal. The project was about changing attitudes towards finance by making invisible information comprehendible.

But design also matters because it is unconditional: ethics are our concern whereas design just supplies us with the tools to make our dreams and fantasies real. As the adage goes, "guns don't kill, people do", so controversial designs like the 3D-printed gun, the designs for which were freely distributed by their designer until banned by the US government, and Massoud Hassani's more obviously beneficial landmine clearing device (see Chapter 9), show us that design can work against and for the common good, depending on your standpoint.

Design matters because it gives us universal languages that can foster our communication with, and understanding and acceptance of, one another. It

BELOW:
Current table
Designed by Marjan van Aubel, UK, 2014

RIGHT:
The Comedy Carpet, Blackpool
Designed by Gordon Young and Why Not Associates, UK, 2011

LEFT:
The Café of Equivalent$
Designed by Kennard Phillipps,
UK, 2009

BELOW:
Liberator 3D-printed gun
Designed by Cody Wilson,
USA, 2013

can bring peace. Design can be used divisively, but it is most potent when it emphasizes our shared humanity and values. Austrian typographer Titus Nemeth designed the Nassim typeface for both Arabic and Latin scripts so that they appear harmonious when they are used together, going some way towards bridging the rift between eastern and western cultures. It is used by the BBC World Service for its Arabic web services.

Design matters because it is a way we can wonder about the future. Revital Cohen's Life Support project speculated about the nature of healthcare and what we may or may not find ethically acceptable. She did not mean it as a genuine proposal to improve healthcare, but rather as the means to consider it.

Last of all, design matters because it is how we will form the world of the future. We should use our understanding of design to see our own pitfalls, such as our greed and shortsightedness, to ensure that the future is more sustainable than the present. Politics only gives us rhetoric, economics gives us structure (sometimes to resist), but it is design that gives us the shape and expression of our hopes for the future.

Compagni avanti, il gran Partito
<small>Nassim Extrabold</small>

Es rettet uns kein höh'res Wesen, kein Gott, kein Kaiser, noch Tribun
<small>Nassim Italic</small>

يكفي عزاء بالخيال علينا العبء
<small>Nassim Regular</small>

assassinés
<small>Nassim Bold</small>

Enternasyonal'le Kurtulur
<small>Nassim Regular</small>

غد الامميه يوحد البشر اسيادنا المستثمرونا
<small>Nassim Regular</small>

wacht auf Verdammte dieser Erde
<small>Nassim SemiBold</small>

comrades
<small>Nassim Regular</small>

nous qui n'étions rien, soyons tout
<small>Nassim Italic</small>

عمال للنضال ففي ييننا الخلاص
<small>Nassim Bold</small>

la Internacional serà el gendre humà!
<small>Nassim Regular</small>

 On kurjan kurjat kunniassaan raharuhtinaat nuo röyhkeät
<small>Nassim Bold</small>

LEFT:
Nassim typeface
Designed by Titus Nemeth,
Austria, 2007

BELOW:
Life Support
Designed by Revital Cohen,
UK, 2008

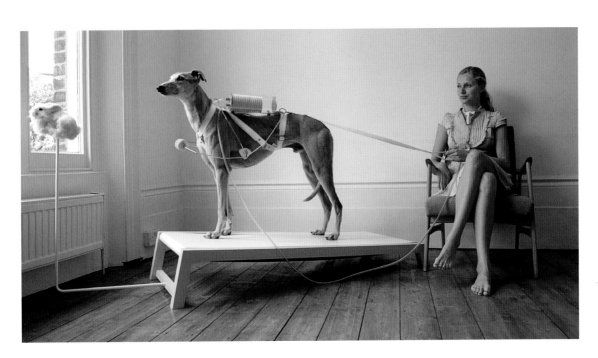

GLOSSARY

This list contains definitions of some terms associated with the design process, but not an exhaustive glossary of materials and techniques. For further information, see Further Reading.

Additive manufacturing

Additive manufacturing is the term used to describe 3d printing techniques that gradually add layers of material until the object is completed. See Chapter 8.

Arts and Crafts

The Arts and Crafts movement originated in Britain in the later part of the nineteenth century and found influence in America and Europe. Under the guidance of designers and artists such as William Morris and Edward Burne-Jones, the movement celebrated hand-workmanship, craftsmen and an ideal of rural life as an antidote to the rise in city-living and cheap factory-made goods. Arts and Crafts designers were often aligned with left-wing politics, even though their products remained expensive and unavailable to ordinary people. The aims of the movement influenced modernist design in the twentieth century through design schools such as the Bauhaus in Germany.

Bauhaus

The Bauhaus was an extremely influential art and design school in Germany in the 1920s and 1930s that promoted modernist design ideas.

Biomimicry

Biomimicry is the imitation of the models, principles and systems of the natural world in order to resolve human problems. It is not the same as naturalism in art, which would depict a flower as it appears realistically. Rather, biomimicry generates structures controlled by the principles governing how plants grow, without them needing to look like copies of plants. The organic world of plants and animals are popular sources of inspiration for designers, as are less visible geological and even chemical structures that may be mimicked in the design of synthetic materials. See also Exoskeleton.

Computer-aided design

CAD, or computer-aided design, software lets designers work with exact dimensions and see their ideas in 2D or 3D form, and from any angle. CAD substantially speeds up the design process and gives designers technical information about the strength or flexibility of their design.

Creative Commons

Creative Commons licenses do not replace copyright but are based on it. They allow designers to specify exactly which rights they wish to retain, and which they will share free of charge. The result is a low-cost, low-overhead copyright management system. Creative Commons licenses were conceived in 2001. See also Open Source and Chapter 12.

Design for disassembly

In order to maximize the opportunity to re-use or recycle components and materials in complex products, it is important that they are designed for disassembly at the end of their useful life. This requires designers and manufacturers to consider how they are assembled in the first place. Laminating processes and most glues permanently fix components together whereas versatile threaded fixings can be removed to separate parts made of different materials.

Ergonomics

Also known as 'human-centred design' ergonomic design focuses on the relationship of the human body to its environment and aims to maximize comfort and ease of use. By putting the user first, ergonomics influences the design of tools, kitchen appliances, furniture, interior design and even social spaces. Applied to furniture design, ergonomic principles demand that chairs are adjustable to suit all body types to ensure not only comfort, but the reduction of the risk of strain through poor posture. See Chapters 7 and Chapter 10.

Exoskeleton
Unlike mammals, which have their skeletons concealed within their bodies, insects and crustaceans have their structures, known as exoskeletons, on the outside. The idea influences designers and architects, who put the structures of their works visibly on the outside edge to free up space on the inside. See also Biomimicry.

Flat-pack
Flat-pack, also known as ready-to-assemble or knock-down furniture, applies the principle of modular design to the problem of furniture. By reducing the number of components and considering how they can be fitted together most easily, often with fittings that are usable in many different contexts, designers and manufacturers of flat-pack furniture can greatly reduce their costs. This is partly because furniture can be shipped more economically and also because the costs and effort of assembly are passed to the end user. Michael Thonet pioneered the principles of flat-pack furniture with his steam-bent chairs in the mid-nineteenth century, but it became ubiquitous in the hands of Swedish furnishing giant IKEA from the 1950s. See also Modular Design and Chapter 5.

Globalism
Globalism is the attitude or policy of placing the interests of the entire world above those of individual nations. In design terms, globalism refers to products that lack a local identity deriving from the place where they are made, and that are traded all over the world. Training shoes are a good example of a globalized product: to an extent so are cars. Critics of globalism feel it destroys local cultures and differences. See Chapter 5.

Hacking
In design terms, hacking means adapting or customizing an existing design to improve it or change its role. See Chapter 12.

Localism
In terms of design, localism is the will to make and consume products locally, within a community, using locally sourced materials and maintaining a sense of local specificity and culture. It is a response to the effects of globalism, which provides identical products for everyone, everywhere. See Chapter 5.

Mass production
This is the term used to describe the system of making many multiples of a design in a factory setting, in order to reduce costs and increase volumes.

Modernism
In the early twentieth century, a rejection of past styles and a belief in technological progress influenced art, design and culture. Buildings, products and furniture, it was thought, should clearly express their functions rather than concealing them behind decoration.

Modular design
This design approach regards products as assemblages of different units that could be reconfigured in different systems to achieve other results. For example cars, high-rise buildings and computers all incorporate modular components that can be updated or replaced where necessary. Modular design has the benefit of lower cost through mass production while still allowing for the customization of products. See also Flat-pack.

Open source design
As it implies, open source designs are those that are free and open for anyone to access. Open

source principles emerged first in the design and distribution of free computer software that was customized, embellished, improved and shared for free by numerous users. Having numerous authors made some of this software more resilient than proprietary software developed by fewer engineers. Open source designs are alternatives to designs protected by copyright that are the property of designated owners who can choose to license their use to third parties, often for a fee. Individuals can also choose to publish completed and resolved work as open source designs. See also Creative Commons and Chapter 12.

Parametrics

In design, parametrics refers to the setting of parameters and boundaries that will affect the outcome, most often in terms of computer-aided design software systems, for example algorithms that will generate curves or compute structures with the optimal weight-to-strength ratio. Software will also compute the effect on one parameter setting if another is altered. See also Computer-aided design and Chapter 8.

Planned obsolescence

In the 1950s, designers and marketers realized that they could promote more sales of products if they changed their appearances seasonally according to fashion. The notion became commonplace in the automobile industry but spread to other sectors such as kitchen appliances like refrigerators. Rather than designing a car or a fridge to last as long as possible, they were designed with the idea that they would soon go out of fashion and their owner would wish to replace them with the latest model, even if they were not yet worn out. Another way to encourage consumers to replace their products was to design components that would quickly fail. See Chapter 4.

Postmodernism

Postmodernism, a stylistic period from the 1970s to the 1990s, was a reaction against the uniformity of modernist design and affected architecture, furniture, industrial design, fashion and graphics. Designers plundered historical styles and freely mixed references from high culture and popular culture (for example mixing Greek classical architectural orders with references to Disney cartoons). The modernist credo that 'form follows function' was replaced with the tongue-in-cheek 'form follows fun'.

Prototype

A prototype is a full-scale working version of a new design, made to test it. Because they are often complex and made as one-offs, they can be very expensive for technical products, but they are a necessary part of the design process. See Chapters 1 and 2.

Retro-styling

If a product's appearance is made to look like it is from an earlier era, it has been retro-styled. Each era has its own distinctive design signature depending on fashion and technological developments, and alluding to these features gives new products a sense of history and appeals to consumers' nostalgia. See Chapter 4.

Styling

How a product looks and feels, depending on the materials used to make it and the combination of colours, textures, patterns and balance of shapes within it, is often known as styling. Styling is about the external appearance of a product, rather than its inner workings or ability to function well. See Chapter 4.

Sustainability

Sustainable systems and processes are those that can endure over time. In design terms these are systems and processes that balance ecology and economics. More specifically, sustainable design is taken to mean design and manufacturing that does not adversely harm the environment through over-use of irreplaceable natural resources or through pollution. See Chapter 9.

FURTHER READING

Braungart, Michael and McDonough, William; *Cradle to Cradle, Re-making the Way We Make Things, 2002*

Design Museum, *Designs of the Year*, catalogues for 2008-2014

Fiell, Charlotte and Fiell, Peter; *Plastic Dreams, Synthetic Visions in Design*, 2009

Fiell, Charlotte and Fiell, Peter, *The Story of Design*, 2013

Gershenfeld, Neil; *Fab: The Coming Revolution on your Doorstep – from Personal Computers to Personal Fabrication*

Lefteri, Chris; *Making It, Manufacturing Techniques for Product Design*, 2012

Olivares, Jonathan; *A Taxonomy of Office Chairs*, 2011

Phaidon Design Classics, 2006

Schwartzman, Madeline; *See Yourself Sensing, Redefining Human Perception*, 2011

Sudjic, Deyan (General Editor); *Design in Britain*, 2009

Thompson, Martin and Thompson, Rob; *Sustainable Materials, Processes and Production*, 2013

Williams, Gareth; *21 Twenty-one, 21 Designers for Twenty-first Century Britain*, 2012

ACKNOWLEDGEMENTS

Thank you to Charlotte and Peter Fiell for suggesting that I write this book in the first place and for their comments on the content and the final manuscript. Thank you to Helen Charman at the Design Museum for her enthusiastic support and advice regarding content. Thanks to Gemma Maclagan Ram at Carlton for steering the project. Thank you to Ed Barber and Jay Osgerby, Mark Miodovic, Daniel Charny, the Design Museum Designs of the Year organisers and all the others who knowingly - or unknowingly - have fed me ideas. Many thanks to all the designers and manufacturers who have supplied images of their work for inclusion in this book, and who have shown me the important ways that design matters. Lastly, many many thanks to Richard Sorger.

INDEX

Italic type refers to illustrations or their captions.

CREDITS

The publishers would like to thank the following sources for their kind permission to reproduce the pictures in this book.

Key: t=Top, b=Bottom, m=Middle, l=Left and r=Right.

Page 4 MYTO; **8** Gear Wrench; **9** Design by Ben Wilson & Jonathan Pooley, photography by John Selby; **11** Castledown Type Family by The Entente & Colophon Foundry. Commissioned by Neil Small; **12** Courtesy of Shephard Fairey/ObeyGiant.com; **13** Benjamin Hennig www.londonmapper.org.uk; **15** © ROLI Ltd, 2014; **16** Eone Timepieces; **19-21** KGID; **23-29** Barber Osgerby; **31** BEPictured/Shutterstock; **32** Private Collection; **33** Private Collection; **34** Original1227™©Anglepoise®; **35** Anglepoise® Fifty by Anthony Dickens; **36** Tiago da Fonseca; **37** Pizzakobra, iGuzzini. Design by Ron Arad; **38** Wiki; **39l** Naoto Fukasawa Design; **39r** Industrial Facility www.retailfacility.co.uk; **40** Sipa Press/Rex Features; **41** Brompton Bicycle, photography by Peter Hughs; **44t** Nissan; **44b** I studio/Alamy; **45t** Rich Niewiroski Jr/Wikimedia Commons; **45m** Wiki; **45b** wiki; **46l** © Marek Novotny & Qubus; **46r** Wagado; **47** Vibol Moeung/Plumen; **48** Dualit; **49** Alamy; **51** Hayonstudio; **52** Getty Images; **54- 55** www.sugru.com; **56** Dominic Wilcox; **57** Re-Do Studio; **58** Thomas Thwaites; **59** Thonet GmbH Frankenberg; **60 - 61** Pipal; **63 - 65** Will Shannon; **67l** Condensed Matter Physics Group at University of Manchester; **67r** Mauricio Affonso; **68** Masaya Yoshimura; **69** Design by Kihyun Kim, photo by Jiah Kim; **70** Seongyong Lee; **71** Benjamin Hubert; **72t** Bendywood; **72b** Petr Krejci; **73** Tatiana Uzlova; **74t** Paper Pul Helmet, Tom Gottelier, Edward Thomas and Bobby Petersen; **74b** Ariane Prin; **75t** Jair Straschnow; **75b** Artek; **77** Studio Hansje; **78** Kyocera; **79** Courtesy of Lovegrove Studio; **80t** Katharina Kayser; **80b** Wendelin Schulz-Pruss; **81t** ALBI SERFATY; **81b** Vessel; **82** Paley Studios Archive; **83t** Barber Osgerby; **83b** Hansgrohe; **84t** Tord Boontje; **84b** designed by Jólan van der Wiel, photographed by Jac van der Wiel; **85t** Heatherwick Studios; **85b** Photography by Peter Mallet; **86** György K rössy/Barber Osgerby; **87 - 88** Photo by John Ross courtesy of Lovegrove Studio; **89t** Tom Dixon & Jack Fluoro; **89b** Made in Mind www.madeinmind.co.uk; **90t** Silo Studio 2011; **90b** Surface Table, 2008; designed by Terence Woodgate & John Barnard for Established & Sons; **91** Melissa Shoes; **92t** Simon Peers & Nicholas Godley; **92b** Images courtesy of Moritz Waldermeyer; **93t** Mischer'traxler studio; **93b** Anton Alvarez; **94** Casper Sejersen; **95t** Nendo, photographed by Masayuki Hayashi; **95b** Yasuhiro Suzuki Recocoon; **96** Rick Friedman/rickfriedman.com/Corbis; **97t** BMW; **97b** Rowan Mersh; **99** Wetcake Studio/Getty Images; **100** Future Publishing/Rex Features; **101t** Johnny Kelly/Barber Osgerby; **101b** Konstantin Grcic, Waver, for Vitra. Photo Marc Eggimann © Vitra; **102t** Designed by Renfrew Group International for the National Innovation Centre; **102b** Ericlarson + rickybiddle; **103** www.carbonblacksystem.com; **104** Dr David Swann, Reader in Design, University of Huddersfield; **105** PEARSONLLOYD; **106** Stratasys; **107** Goodwin Hartshorn; **108** Eyewriter; **109** Simon Kinneir; **111l** Designed by Bathsheba Grossman for MGX by Materialise; **111r** Wiki; **113** Matthew Plummer-Fernandez; **114t** WinSun; **114b** 3D Systems; **115** Grace Choi, Mink; **116t** Images courtesy of Drs. Li Wen, James Weaver & George Lauder; **116b** Jake Evill; **117** 3Doodler; **119** Lindsey Hoshaw; **120** Studio Swine & Kieran Jones, photography by Juriaan Booij; **121** Alfredo Moser; **122** Design by Jon Bohmer, Kyoto Energy Ltd; **123** Massoud Hassani; **124** ©Joerg Boethling/Alamy; **125** Photo courtesy of Professor Ido Bruno & Arthur Brutter; **126t** Re-Do Studio; **126b** Fairphone; **127** William West/Getty Images; **129l** Levi Strauss UK Limited; **129r** Jitesh Jagadish/Flickr; **130l** Alexander Johmann/Flickr; **130r** ©IanDagnall Computing/Alamy; **131l** Kate Moss logo, 2007, Art Director Peter Saville, Designer Paul Barnes, after the typeface Albro designed by Alexander Brodovitch, PLINC, New York; **131r** Designed by: Mode Project and Sender. Mode Project: Colin Carter, Principal; Steve Juras, Creative Director. Sender, LLC: Sol Sender, Principal; Amanda Gentry, Designer; Andy Keene, Designer. **132** London Stereoscopic Company/Getty Images; **133l** Ian Jackson/The London Bus Museum; **133r** The London Bus Museum; **135b** Badudoy/Wikimedia Commons; **135b** Bob Walker/Wikimedia Commons; **136** Heatherwick Studio; **137t** View Pictures/Getty Images; **137b** View Pictures/Getty Images; **138** United States Patent and Trademark Office; **139l** www.vitra.com; **139r** Bonhams; **140** Herman Miller; **141** Humanscale; **142** © Magis, photo by Tom Vack; **143** Knoll, Inc; **145l** Wilkhaln Ltd. Design by ProductEntwicklung Roericht, Burkhard Schmitz, Franz Biggel; **145r** Herman Miller; **146t** © 2014 Atari Interactive, Inc; **146bl** Wikimedia; **146br** © 2014 Atari Interactive, Inc; **147** Nintendo; **148-49** Playstation; **150** Microsoft; **151l** Nintendo; **151r** PhotoAlto/Alamy; **152** Converse; **153-56** Nike; **157** Adidas; **158** Puma; **159** Nike; **160** Patrick Gries; **161** David Paul Morris/Getty Images; **163** Bloomua/Shutterstock; **164-65** Dyson; **166-67** Google; **169** Commissioned for Bloomberg Philanthropy by art and design agency Arts Co, 'Waste Not, Want It' is a series of specially commissioned art and design projects made almost entirely out of Bloomberg's waste.; **171** Lou Rihn; **172** Re-Do Studio; **173** Fixperts; **174** Bloomberg/Getty Images; **175** Unfold, photography by Kristof Vrancken; **176-77** courtesy of F.A.T. Lab & Sy-Lab; **178** Formlabs; **179** Make Magazine; **181** SolidSpace; **182** Matthijs Labadie; **183** A work of art by Gordon Young designed in collaboration with Why Not Associates; **184t** Kennardphillipps; **184b** Cody Wilson; **185t** Titus Nemeth; **185b** Cohen Van Balen.

Every effort has been made to acknowledge correctly and contact the source and/or copyright holder of each picture and Carlton Books Limited apologises for any unintentional errors or omissions, which will be, corrected in future editions of this book.